TO ALEX
ENJOY TH
BRUCE

TO HELL AND BACK

BRUCE CADOGAN

aka Rodney Bruce

ACKNOWLEDGEMENTS

To the profound influences in my life; my mother Hazel, my grandparents mama and papa, my uncle Norris and my friend Rodney, who died too young.
To my friend Sandra, your inputs were invaluable, thank you
To my sister Sonia, I did it finally, thanks for encouraging me.
To my daughter Tyra, thank you for your constant advice.
To my sister Dawn, a big thanks for the long hours and guidance in putting this book together.
To Nina and the rest of my writing class, thank everyone in our little group for their contribution in helping me to grow as a writer
To my family and dearest friends, thank you. I love you all

TABLE OF CONTENTS

1

PART 1

CONSCIOUSLY BLACK

THE FREEDOM FIGHTERS

10

Woke this morning and forgot to breathe,
Smelled the flowers, saw two dozen wreathes,
Don't want to die but I've got no reason to live,
Don't want to cry but I've got nothing to give.
Born living on the edge of tomorrow,
No where to live, no food to borrow.
Hunger has no class, colour, religion or race,
All we have ever asked is respect and to manage our own space.

Is it in my mind or is this so damn senseless?
Why do they target the poor, the ones that are defenseless?
Feel so lost in this barren land,
Cannot see my feet, cannot feel my hands.
Something has happened; I do not want to cry,
I am only twenty-one but I am ready to die.

I remember school days, we were told to focus,
On their false lies, they tried to choke us.
Now I live my life through the hands of my enemy,
My God, my God, my God, what have you done to me?
Went from the teachings of the Bible to the Quran,
Only to realize that right is the right and wrong is wrong.
Where is the love I was promised when I was born?
Another funeral service, another day to mourn.

THE FREEDOM FIGHTERS

Although this land for us has no plans,
We will defend it until we die using bottles, sticks and cans.
Some are lost in desperation; some are lost in hate,
The world is getting smaller but still no food on my plate
As another night and the violence unfolds,
Will my brother or my sister live to reach ten years old?

I think of those who are less blessed,
The motherless, the fatherless!
There is no silver lining, no velvet rope,
Father please help them, as they have no way to cope.
As another rocket lights up the sky,
We are not worthy; we are simply born to die.
We have trespassers commanding our land,
Our daily existence is through their commands.

Although I cannot see my feet, cannot feel my hands,
I will die for our freedom on our own land.
They use politics and mind games,
Even murder us in our slumber to fulfill their aims,
I cry freedom in my deepest sleep,
It is my only hope that I beg you to keep.

12

I LIVED IN MY SKIN

I lived in my skin
I cried in my skin
I lived in my skin
I died in my skin.

Chased on mounted steeds,
From people carrying acts of evil deeds,
Welcomed you with open arms,
Closed our eyes,
Fell to your spell using your charms,
Woke to find it was nothing but lies!
Taken from homes in bottomless ships,
Mastered by chains and angry whips,
Too few made the journey here,
When chained in ships with no inches to spare.
Women, sold for their fertility,
Men, sold for their virility.

Committed nature's sin,
Kept me in chains because of my skin,
Greed grew, forsaken our health,
Off our backs, they made their wealth.
In the burning sun, we worked all day,
We lived to work, 'til we passed away.
To our fallen soldiers, their memories we must preserve
Justice will be served
When they get what they deserve.

I LIVED IN MY SKIN

Even if I wanted,
I could not change the fact,
You could not accept me as a man,
All you could see was that I'm black.
I lived in my skin, I cried in my skin,
I was blessed here first,
Who God blessed,

Let no man curse.
I lived in my skin,
I died in my skin.

I felt my fears and anger dried my tears,
I wonder if this will end in the next four hundred years.
Father, my Father, I asked you for help,
But this is what you gave,
Lord, I question your reason for making me brave.
Born as a man, but lived as a child,
Freedom came, with my ashes spreading wild.
Took our religion and gave it back,
Removed all the facts that the creator is black.

I lived in my skin,
I cried in my skin,
I lived in my skin; and
I died in my skin.

SCARS

I wear my scars,
I have nothing to hide.
I hold my head high and I walk with pride,
I carry the scars of 400 years of slavery,
I wear the scars of 400 years of bravery.
Some will say they understand how I feel,
How can they?
They've never walked in my shoes?

I remember the days I worked for nothing,
I said nothing.
That was music to your ears and coppers to your pockets.
I wear my scars,
I have nothing to hide,
I hold my head high and I walk with pride.
As long as I'm alive and my voice can be heard,
I will keep talking, as I am not yet battle weary.

Do not think because of the thoughts that I leak,
That I am someone who is sad, lonely or desperately weak.
I do not celebrate misery,
Nor do I dance in the theme of unhappiness.
I need to get this mentality shifted
Show the world how truly we have been gifted.
There are days when I sit and reflect,
Of the things that I see and others neglect.
I ask questions to myself,
I look for answers from no one else.

SCARS

We worked to the theme of your whips,
We died to the sound of your guns,
Children in your cotton fields from age of walking,
Built your future dying in the sugar fields,
Stripped naked and sold as seen for your profits,
Paraded and fought for your pleasure,
Died fighting your wars you created.

After 400 years we no longer wish to do this!
I hear voices defining us as lazy,
We simply no longer wish to work for nothing.
The desire for greed, fueled by hate.
Was only surpassed by your lack of humanity.

I wear my scars,
I have nothing to hide,
I wear my scars,
I walk with my head held high,
I walk with pride.

16

NEW WORLD ORDER

We live in a world of new world order,
Bridges have been burned, so few borders.
Cut me deep!
See the colour I bleed,
On your hospital bed,
Is this the blood that you need?
We have one life to live,
The truth is all we have to give.

They say my ideas are fundamentally flawed,
Some of my ideas should be outlawed,
Still it is just a wish; it is a thought, a dream.
Are my ideas really so extreme?
Look past my colour and see my features,
For underneath, we are all God's creatures.

The feeble controls the mass,
Each day they present new laws to pass.
Show me a minister at a battlefront,
Then I will show you a picture that is just a photo stunt.
Forget the racism, the "isism" and the "schisms",
Bouts of nepotism!
As a people, we have achieved much,
We have come so far,
It is not about who we were,
It is about now, who we are.

They tell me peace is in heaven, none on earth,
Does that mean my life has so little value, so little worth?
I see things that are wrong, fundamental and monumental,
They say Bruce you are crazy, you are totally mental.
I wonder when will God allow people to be themselves?
No more sitting down with thoughts like empty shelves.

We live in a world of new world order,
Bridges have been burned, so few borders.
The White House had a real cool resident,
He was black, and he was the president.

The man born without vision uses other senses than his sight,
He will see more than you and yet you challenge his rights.
Everybody talk,
You talk to him,
I talk to her,
See, when we turn off the lights,
We are all the same colour.
As a people, we can achieve whatever we want,
So do not let them smile at you and tell you that you can't.
We live in a world of new world order,
Bridges have been burned,
So few borders,
Cut me deep see the colour I bleed,
But on your hospital bed,
Is this the blood that you need?

NEW WORLD ORDER

18

SO LOST IN YOUR COUNTRY

I am so lost I cannot be found,
If I were a dog, I would probably be a hound.
I have a dream, I have a wish
One day my children and I will share a dish.

From the ashes of my dreams,
Each night I hear my people scream,
Do you wonder why I ask you to marry me?
So I could stay safe and live in your country.
Didn't come to your land to start a rift,
But your freedom, your freedom is such a gift.
I am so hungry, I am so broke.
If I did not laugh: on this fresh air, I would probably choke.

I feel I am the missing link,
I am in your thoughts for less than a blink,
I could be a woman, I could be a man,
I could be from Syria, Libya, Cambodia or Iran.

You have strangled my voice,
To steal, you have put me in a position where I have no choice.
How can I trust someone else?
When I have a problem simply trusting myself?
In my country, I am hunted with a price on my head,
The prize is happiness on their faces when they see that I am dead.
I do not begrudge you for what you've got,
So please, do not judge me for what I have not.

I have no wish to be rude,
I have no wish to be crude,
But you complain when you see my face,
I bet you would not swap my place.

I am you without a voice,
I am you without a choice,
I have no rights unless I die
So 'til then on this pauper's grave I will lie.

20

HATE

I hate you for hating my skin
I hate you for all the pain that you bring.
I hate you for killing my friend,
I do not know when this pain will end.
I hate you because to live, so many times I have to beg,
I hate having to catch up using just on one leg.
I hate you because you cannot see the pain I am living in
And because you would kill twice if I had a twin.

I hate you for stealing my name,
Then you tell me for all of my troubles, that I am to blame.
I hate you for killing my fathers and my brothers,
For the sins against my sisters and mothers.
I hate that you do not acknowledge what you've done,
You kill us when we sleep or even when we run.
I hate that years ago we had to ask to remove a slave master's statue
Time and time again,
We were told,
The decision is still under review.

I hate that you have no idea,
What it is to live in this country in my skin,
You see my colour as a sin.
I hate that I have to tell you that black lives matter
When I know the poor gets leaner and the rich gets fatter.
I hate that we have tried everything year after year,
And now I can see your hate, now that you are living in fear.

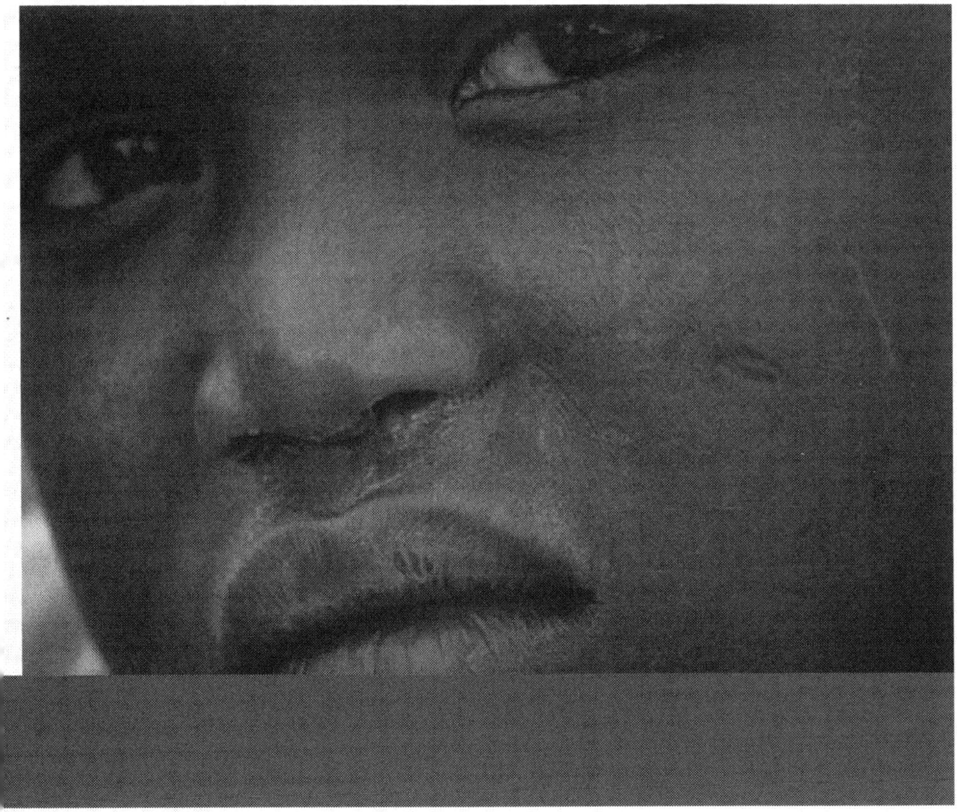

HATE

22

MY WORLD

I was born with my eyes open,
Born fighting for tomorrow,
Do you know how many lives
I've had to borrow?
Another corpse is born,
Another family is torn,
Another funeral service,
Another family is broken,
Yeah, yeah it is just another token!
See, we do not die one by one,
We die by the dozen.
Last month, it was my friend,
This week it is my cousin,
He lived and died in honour
He died protecting his manor.

Lived eighteen years on this street,
Never seen a PC on this beat.
Living this life is a certain bet,
That no one has made it to twenty-one as of yet.
We live in a world, where rape is no shame,
It is just another way of making a claim.

Surrounded by mistrust
Hatred, greed and lust
I see no hope, no future, and no family life,
When a vengeful knife can end a peaceful life.
Skanking politicians with their practice smile and their Ray-Ban eyes
They speak so much shit you can smell their lies,
No more begging, begging you please,
No I'd rather die on my feet than live on my knees.
You look at me and wonder where I've lived and where I've been,
Welcome to my world,
This is all I've known since I was in my teens.

MY WORLD

24

IF IT EVER STOPS RAINING

If it ever stops raining
They will see the world I am living in.
No more excuses from all open invitations
Now I will have to give an explanation.
How many years has the rain been my friend?
Is this all for me, is this where the story will end?
Can't imagine laughing with someone else
No, I am happy being here by myself.
The years in truth have left their scars,
Think I'd have made more friends
If I had been living on Mars.

If it ever stops raining
Guess I will learn to keep the pain in.
Wonder if they will notice my practice smile?
Is Tony Curtis still the man in style?
Found living on my own is not all bad
Don't want anyone to make me happy, to make me glad.
Still got that wedding dress, though it doesn't fit any more
People used to say he looked like a young Roger Moore.
In my heart, he will never grow old,
No son, no daughter, no story to be told.

If it ever stops raining in my heart,
I still wonder why the angels took my love away,
On that bright sunny day on the first of May.
Some say he was an angel borrowed to me,
I wonder if it is time, I should let his memories be free.
We never made those trips to any far away land
So many years and yet I still find it hard to cope or understand
Will it ever stop raining in my heart?

IF IT EVER STOPS RAINING

NEW DAY

I do not understand why
I have to struggle all of my life to be equal to you
See, I am not talking to you,
No not directly, but you get my point.
There was the old way
This is a new way, a new day.

Some will try to resist,
Others will persist
Many will say this is foul play
But they have had their day

It is a fact,
The poorest people in the world are either brown or black.
Listen, every man is born free,
But some become enslaved,
Let no one tell you your people were born as slaves.
To that new found God that we've been sold
To him we've been told we must pray,
Well I know that is not our God,
We must change our prayers
To a God that looks like us.
This is a new way
This is a new day.

If we do not water our dreams, they will never grow,
If you do not follow our visions, we will never know.
If Africa had one King or one Queen,
How powerful would we be seen?

NEW DAY

Take back all our stolen lands,
From so-called teachers, lying preachers.
No more pirates, robbers, gravediggers,
Melanin-free full of hate and greed,
Doing whatever they wished to fulfill their glory.
Now they refuse to make a simple apology.

When they came to Africa,
They made us pray by day and they stole by night.
My people, stop, look around, learn and realise,
Treated as slaves, enslaved, and dehumanized.
They robbed from the young, the old and the graves,
Did their best to erase our culture.
They killed, pilfered, treated it as an island that was lost,
Everything they took was to our cost.
Let us take control of our lives and manage our lands,
Give it to our future; put it in our children's hands.

No more past masters laws,
Take control of our country back,
No more strangers coming at will,
Doing, taking whatever they want.
Put a stop to this!
Shut the door!
Throw away the key!

Understand,
We came from the cradle of humankind,
We were the original, the first of all kinds.
I want to stay in a state of reflectiveness,
Not in a state of blind forgiveness,
Not just to live in a house with beautiful flowers,
But to take back what is rightfully ours.
I know we have a long road to travel,
Many deep rivers to cross,
I accept and understand on the way,
Some of our people will get lost.
This is a new way
This is a new day.

28

BAMBOO WALK

Each step that I take is a man by me,
But it seems, a boy by you.

Jumping to your beck-and-call,
You lied to me,
I lied to myself.
You came with the book in exchange for our land,
Told us of your heaven, we did not see your plan.

Names and chains of submission,
Tied to the post I did not weep,
Lashes unforgotten,
Skin ripped, torn, body mutilated.

Hatred you sowed,
Impossible to forget,
Digest the pain you caused,
I am beautiful, one day I will be free,
I am the black butterfly.

I speak not pretty, no laughter lines today,
Eyes missing, tongue removed, shapeless faces,
Black bodies swinging on branches of the sycamore tree.

Stenches on hanged ropes
Skin tarred across continents.

How many millions drowned?
How many millions filled the bellies of whales?
Voices pointlessly screaming, begging for mercy,
Why is this not mentioned in schools?
I feel their hurt it is DNA'd in me
My people's names unmentioned.

BAMBOO WALK

If today I appear to stand tall,
It is because I stand on the shoulders, the backs, the legs,
The outstretched arms, voices simply pleading,
These are lost in his-story.

Millions of souls never to die in peace,
Skin ripped, neck unattached,
If I dared to challenge a skin lighter than mine.

My wife, my sister, daughter,
My brother, my father,
All tenants of their bodies.

Plantations of breeding farms,
Where unspeakable acts of sons,
Forced to lie with mothers.

Submissive to your corrosive wants,
If you ever knew my deepest thoughts,
My deepest hate,
Will my future generations also die as slaves?

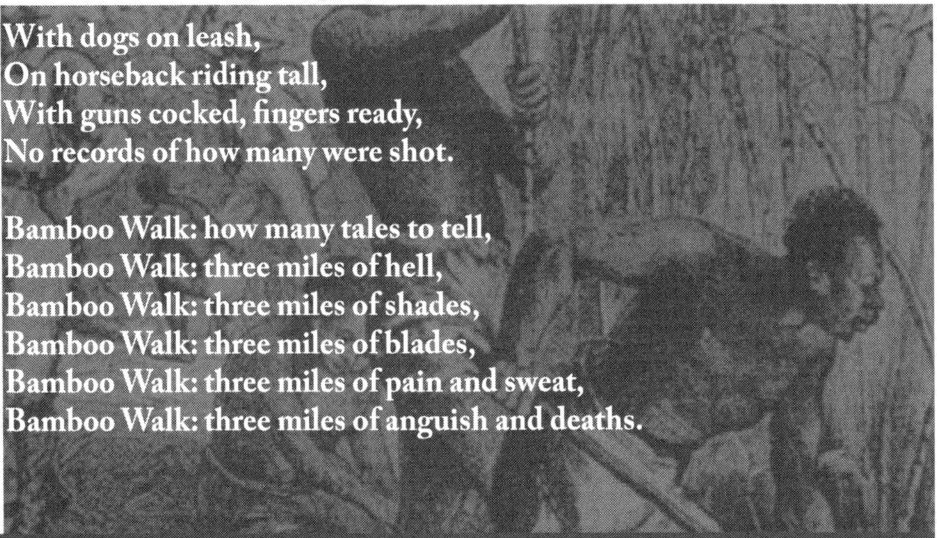

With dogs on leash,
On horseback riding tall,
With guns cocked, fingers ready,
No records of how many were shot.

Bamboo Walk: how many tales to tell,
Bamboo Walk: three miles of hell,
Bamboo Walk: three miles of shades,
Bamboo Walk: three miles of blades,
Bamboo Walk: three miles of pain and sweat,
Bamboo Walk: three miles of anguish and deaths.

30

LEGACY

Do you know real pain is the legacy of lost love?
I cry for the love of my people stolen and lost,
For the legacy of bondage in that invisible chain,
I pray for my people scattered by oceans near and far.

We have survived by having to be strong,
I see those who wish no good, only wrong.
I think in my life I have not been happy but I have been bold,
I am not one who has always done what he has been told.
I am not a perfect role model;
I do not fit that mould.
I speak my mind,
Some people believe that I can be cold.

I speak from the heart and I speak with love,
I see the carnage displayed daily,
Yet we pray and extend forgiveness,
Let us get rid of this 'bear no malice' mentality,
Stand up and be counted!
A change will become an eventuality,
No more celebrating hip hip hooray,
Just because there's no lynching today,
400 years of perfecting the art of forgiveness,
It is not working!

Blacks still dying,
Mothers still crying,
Police are still lying,
How many have ever been charged?
None, they've been put on gardening leave.
Forget Roots, Kunta Kinta or 12 years of slavery,
Put on your tone, then act as if you are brave,
No more crying from baby to grave.
What about the souls and the lives my people gave?
America would not have been built if slavery had never existed,
We would not have survived if we did not fight and at times resisted.

32

I AM, I AM ONE OF YOU

I am, I am one of you!
So many people died in the Iraqi war,
Could you tell me what they were fighting for?
I remember when Obama and Mandela took the oath,
My people some waited a lifetime just to cast their vote.
I felt the shame when Ben Johnson cheated,
Sadly, over the years it's been repeated.

Young brothers come back to the fold,
Before it is too late, before you get too old.
We are standing on the edge, standing on the brink
Come on, come on, use your head, it is time to think.
We have suffered in days before the time of Ramesses
Still suffering, two thousand and twenty, can you picture this?

I feel your hurt of a thousand years,
When no one listened, and no one cares.
When I was a prisoner, I was gagged and bound,
Now I am free, my voice has been found.
That is why I hold my head high, not to the cloud,
But to the highest steeple.
I will not be judged by these jurors,
But only by my rainbow colored people.
I believe in faith,
I believe that love is stronger than hate.

I AM, I AM ONE OF YOU

I am, I am, I am one of you!
Like a circle that has no ends,
It is you who my colour often offends.
For my freedom and my people I will die,
The look in my eyes tells you I speak no lie.
With you, I will share the last food on my plate,
I believe my love is stronger than hate.

No matter how big,
No matter how small,
No matter black or white,
Love conquers all!
For all my people who pretended and had to be brave,
I salute you for all the sacrifice that you gave.

I am, I am, I am one of you!
We do not feel we are part of the pack,
We get a smile in the face and a stab in the back.
They do not see they are overtly racist,
Because we are not shot in all police cases.

When Martin Luther King died,
To my God, now to whom shall we confide?
When Princess Diana died,
The nation cried.
When Stephen Lawrence died,
The police lied!
I am, I am, I am one of you!

BLACK LIVES MATTER

34

I thought our freedom was our blessing,
Maybe we need another lesson.
See, we talk the talk,
We don't always walk the walk.

The world is full of empty promises and cheap drinks,
Do we no longer care how the world sees us?
Do we still care what the world thinks?
In spite of our success, failure and glory,
We end up with the same old story.
Why, do we live to die?
Why do so many mothers need to cry?

Black lives matter,
Do not call this a slave mentality,
Because the slaves before me died so we could live.
I stand before you nearly a broken man,
The weight of my people bears heavily on my shoulders.
Whom should I blame?
Whom should I curse?
My school, my church, the bells that are ringing?

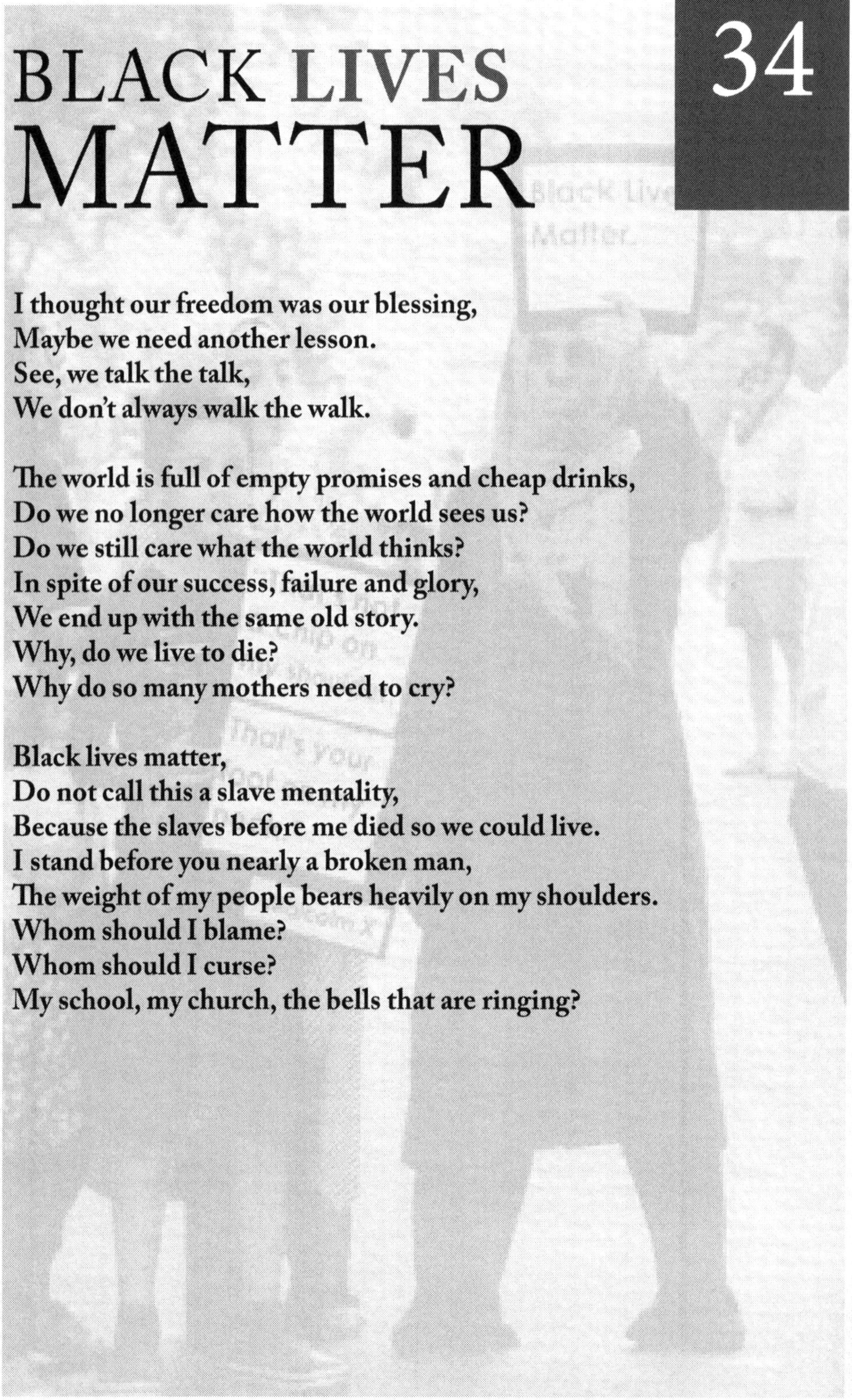

BLACK LIVES MATTER

As I walk with my head bowed,
I am walking with a burdened load,
Now that we are free,
Free to kill ourselves,
Free to kill our dreams.
As another star dies,
Another mother sheds her weeping tears.

Yeah, black lives matter, or so they say,
I am not talking from my rear,
I am talking from my heart, from my eyes,
I am dying, trying to understand the logic of this.
This postcode killing my people, we are taking the piss!

What right would you, you, or you have taking my son's life?
Pardon my anger and pardon my rage,
This senseless killing needs to end.
I have seen my children and their friends
I have seen their fears,
I have seen too many parents shedding tears.
Black lives matter is a fact,
Let's show the world that we are proud and black!

RECOGNITION 36

Seventy-five years on we celebrate on our own,
There will be no stories to mention us or of the planes we had flown.
We came to fight for the motherland,
It was our calling, it was not planned.
Some of us were paid three times less to die
We followed orders and ran to fight and never once questioned why.

We ran into battle and some ran to die?
Told we were needed, I wonder was it a lie?
Today when I look at the celebration pictures I see no black faces,
It's not like the pictures are too big and they have run out of spaces.
But it's ok to die on the battlefields, but not allowed in victory pictures.
The only thing black are the words of the scriptures.

Over a million came to fight for king and country,
Now I look in the mirror and smile and I think yes I did fool me.
To some this may sound like a bitter pill,
Still I fight for the recognition while I have the strength and the will.
If I did not care, I would not mention these facts,
But I still think of my countrymen who never came back.

RECOGNITION

WHY WE MARCH

Let me explain to you why we march,
Before I become tired and my voice becomes parch.
I want my son to walk on any road,
Just like yours,
Without him thinking the colour of his skin is a heavy load.
When you've been sacked from a job for the colour of your skin,
You would know there is a white world and a black world,
The one I am living in.

When I am followed in a shop from isle to isle,
But if I were white,
I would walk all day wearing nothing but a smile.
If I speak up, you tell me to leave and go back home,
Do you realise this world is just one big dome?
To see a brother-man murdered in broad daylight,
There are those who believe its ok, it is all right,
I am trying to explain to you why we march
Before I become tired and my voice becomes parch.

If you've ever been refused accommodation from a dwelling,
And it keeps happening, it is a telling.
When some people are so desperate to fit in,
They go to the lengths of bleaching their skin.
In school days, there was no such thing as black history,
Anything good about black was a total mystery.
When we march and chant I can't breathe, I can't breathe,
Do you hear my anger, do you hear my need?

WHY WE MARCH

I am trying to explain to you why we protest and march,
Before I become tired and my voice becomes parch!
Let me explain to you what is racial profiling,
It is a lawful badge calling me the n' word and still smiling,
I am trying to explain to you why we protest and march
Before I become tired and my voice becomes parch.
You would not understand, in me there is an anger there is a hurt,
If this was a hundred years ago,
You could flog me to death after ripping off my shirt.

**The fact I have to tell you that my life matters,
Shows to the world, the whole system is in tatters.
I am trying to explain to you why we protest and march,
Before I become tired and my voice becomes parch.**

When I think of the killings of Tulsa,
That is why I march.
When I think of the carnage of Sharpeville
That is why I march.
When I think of Stephen Lawrence,
That is why I march.
When I think of Cherry Groce,
That is why I march.
When I think of George Junius Stinney Jr.
That is why we march
When I think of Elijah McClain
That is why I march
When I think of Ahmaud Arbery
That is why I march
When I think of Breonna Taylor,
That is why I march.
When I think of George Floyd,
That is why I march.
When I think of the millions of my people murdered,
That is why I march.
I am marching and searching for peace,
Justice and equality, not revenge,
Otherwise there is no telling how far this would descend.
I am trying to explain to you why we march
Before I come tired and my voice becomes parch.

I CAN'T BREATHE

Three aching words repeated at least 30 times,
They were not said in jest nor in rhymes,
"I can't breathe"
Repeated until life left his soul,
Murdered by those with no care but in control,
Nine minutes 29 seconds of brutality and hate,
Guarded by lackeys, his knee took George Floyd's face.

The world watched and saw his life drained from him,
The cops didn't care they were caught on film.
His voice echoed, I can't breathe! I can't breathe!
Strength gone he could only mime.
My heart felt his need.
He didn't commit a crime but his blackness was a sin,
For 400 years this is the world, blacks have been living in.

The world watched in disbelief, frustration anger and rage.
People refused to close their eyes and simply go to the next page.
Marches started locally,
People came out vocally,
Then the world came out globally,
They realized this is happening socially.
We no longer wish to be pilgrims,
That can wait.
We demand peace justice, not when it is too late.
If it is not given we will fight to the very end,
The choice is yours if you want these fences to mend.
No more sitting down and leaving from an empty table,
Time to stand up, march and do what you are able.
"I can't breathe" repeated at least 30 times,
The dying words of a man as his colour was his crimes.

I CAN'T BREATHE

AMERICA'S TIME TO LEARN

Tick tock, tick tock, tick tock,
Time is running out,
Tick tock, tick tock, tick tock.

The land of hope and glory
That's what they said made America great
Built by the blood of slaves and indigenous people
Fueled by greed they took without asking
For 400 years of cruelty, racism and killings,
They have been dining and we have been fasting.

Another black killing
For you it's another comfortable night's sleep
But for me I want black justice,
Because this goes ancestors deep.
Let me take you to
1918 when Mary Turner had her pregnant belly split open
1921, the Tulsa massacre
An act of racism, hatred, jealousy and greed
1944 George Junius Stinney a boy of 15 executed
pardoned 70 years later
2020 Breonna Taylor shot in her bed
By another race hater.
America this is no mystery.
This is your history.

Tick tock, tick tock, tick tock,
Time is running out,
Tick tock, tick tock, tick tock.

AMERICA'S TIME TO LEARN

America,
We are angry and we are stern!
What will it take for you to
Listen and for you to learn?
We have pain in us that is generations deep,
The kind of pain we wish to share and no longer keep.

Against us, you have committed,
Some of the most hateful crimes
Now it needs to stop,
We believe it is about time.
Peacefully, we tried to remonstrate,
Now it is too late,
We have to march and demonstrate.
Now you want me to stop my actions,
Go to church then go home and sleep,
The pain that is in me goes ancestors deep.

We've taught ourselves to pray
We've even taught our babies to sing.

We tried praying.
We died praying,
We tried running.
We died running,
We tried sleeping.
We died sleeping,
We tried sitting.
We died sitting,
We tried standing.
We died standing,

You have been so used to seeing us dying,
You have been so used to seeing us crying.
To the Karen's of this world,
who used our ethnicity as a weapon,
Then laugh and joke and simply carry on,

People are dying and cities are burning,
People are marching, they will not be quiet,
They will not be turning.
When I saw how George Floyd was killed
A part of me as a human died with him.
The killers would have gotten away with murder,
If it were not caught on film,
Now they procrastinate,
Yet, that only fuels the belly of hate.

Tick tock tick tock tick tock,
America time is running out.
The clock is ticking,
Tick tock tick tock.

AMERICA'S TIME TO LEARN

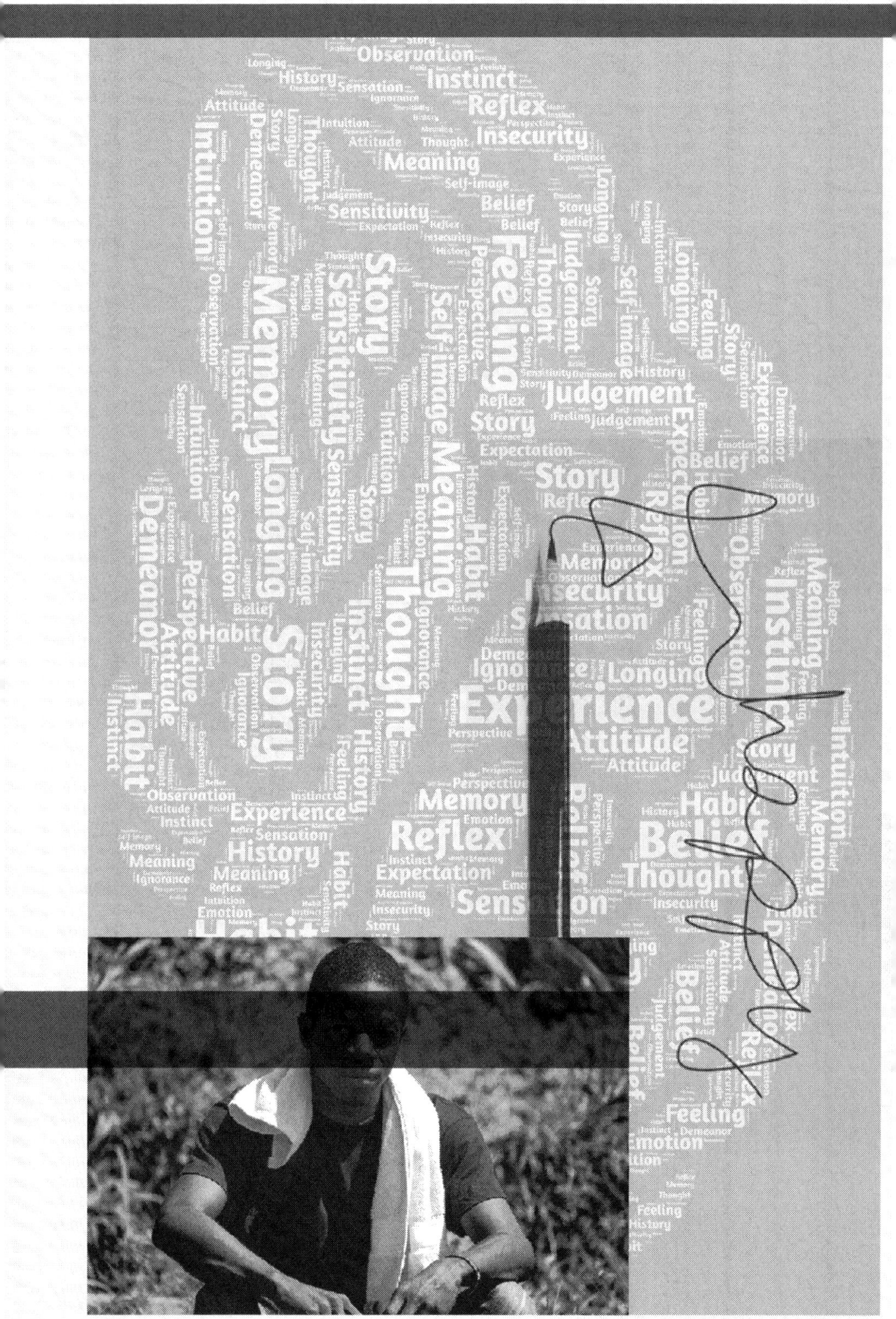
Unhappy

PART 2

MY THOUGHTS IN WORDS

My Thoughts In Words

48

GOD'S TEAM

Another day,
No money at hand for these bills to pay,
Heat or eat, that is my choice today.
I was born on my own,
I can fend for myself.
Feel so weak,
As strong as an elf.

Why can't I be happy and poor?
Life ties you up to always want more.
If I followed my eyes I'd do something wrong,
I listen to you Father to keep me strong.
Times are hard and times are lean,
I am not going to rob,
I am not going to steal.
I have been saved,
I am in God's team.

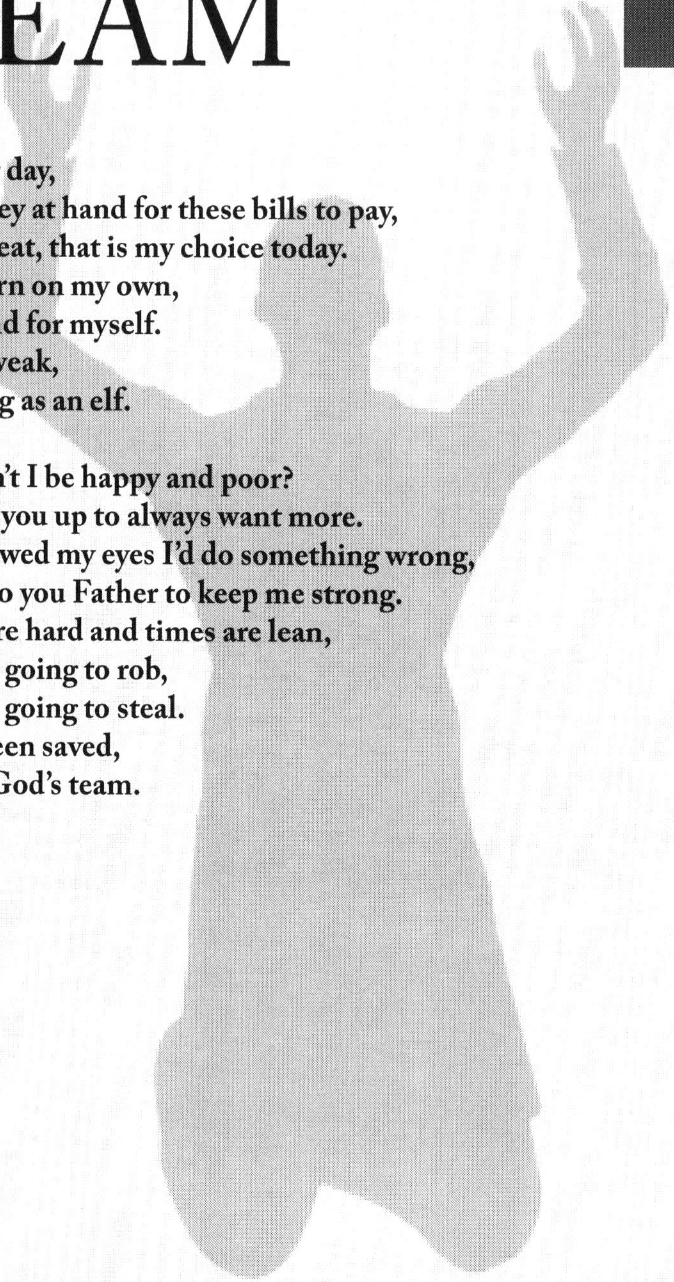

GOD'S TEAM

The pressures of life today,
Sometimes take man from his beliefs,
And makes him stray.
Charity, I have been told begins at home,
Except times are hard and I am so alone.
Your guiding thoughts keep me so right,
Every day is a struggle, every day is a fight.
Only through your eyes, I can be myself,
Won't be judged by someone else.
I have been saved,
I am in God's team.

The angels called and kept my eyes alight,
They gave me strength in my life to fight.
The guns and the knives are just the fool's way,
They had a plan for me, now it is my time to play.
Your will and your words I am here to teach,
To all those just outside your reach.
My pockets are empty and my home is cold,
Though in your hands, I give my life to hold.
Times are hard and times are lean,
I am not going to rob,
I am not going to steal.
I have been saved,
I am in God's team.

LIFE

Life, at times, is like an albatross with no wings,
It is like the garden that has no beauty,
It is that vision lost in time,
It is when forgiveness is impossible to teach.

Life is an unfolding story,
Full of sadness and glory,
Takes you to the tunnel of memories good and bad,
Life stops and starts but has no ending,
If you have no memories of sadness
You should know that you have not lived,
We all have lived with moments of regrets.

LIFE

Memories of shattered dreams,
Too many nights of silent screams.
We search for answers to life,
But wisdom often comes with a price.
Enlightenment sometimes comes too late,
Still we search for answers we cannot find,
Those questions play on our minds.

The road to harmony has many turns, bumps and bruises.
Life is not always perfect
The days when there are too many rivers in your eyes.
You will know it is love if they call and say
I am sorry, I made you cry.

Life is not and never will be fair,
It is not an equal opportunity scheme,
It allows you to get lucky sometimes,
Treasure the moments!

52

I WAS MADE FIRST

I was made first,
Made from dust,
Formed from the ground,
I was made first, pound for pound,
In a slumber mind, I was given a wife,
Made to love her,
To share her pain,
And for her to share my gain.

There was a time of no doctor, no nurse,
I was there, I was made first.
First to question why we die,
Gave myself to make her from me,
My Father blessed me with a love so free,
First to cover her finger with a ring,
Her eyes said yes and my heart did sing.

Men sometimes forget when they are wrong,
Even forgetting her favourite song,
We laugh with you and cry by ourselves,
Men are not supposed to cry with someone else.
Not all men are blessed like the mighty Thor,
But a good man is worth fighting for.

We are the first to go to war,
Some say the last to leave the bar.
It is more than that which makes me a man,
I carry respect even if he is from another clan,
He is not a stranger,
He could be from London, Jamaica or the motherland,
Eye contact we acknowledge Jah fellow man.
The love that we cherish for our newborn,
Silently praising the Father for a new morn.

I WAS MADE FIRST

First words taught: goodbye, thank you and please,
First to say I love you on bended knees.
Not always the first to admit when we are wrong,
Still trying to remember your favourite song.
We sometimes are simple and vain,
Even forget to use our brains,
We hang our hats sometimes too high,
In a challenge to reach the sky.

The simple things we do for fun,
Like headphones blasting on our daily run,
Time bonding at our preferred bar,
Celebrating life with our classic cigar,
Licking our finger from a tasty dish,
Making Halle Berry our favourite wish.

The love and respect to all kinds,
Especially the ones that linger in our minds.
We do not say it often;
We do not say it loud;
We do not say it with feelings;
I have nothing to hide,
I am standing here with nothing but pride.

54

I SPEAK MY MIND

If you look too closely,
You may not like what you find.
In my life,
I have been sad, happy and bold,
I am not one who does exactly as he's been told.
If I were born a slave, many times I would have been sold.
I do not believe I would have lived to be old.

Life is full of promises and endless supposes,
Not every day is pink champagne and red roses.
I see those with ignorance in bright sunshine.
I wonder how long they will last.
I prefer the ones,
who provoke thoughts,
And are willing learners,
Always ready to ask,
My frustrations with life,
Sometimes get the better of me.

I SPEAK MY MIND

YORK

If you ask me to dine,
I am not a diner until you ask me to sit.
So I ask you to sit and celebrate York's 50 years,
Whomsoever you are with.
We honour our founders who fought and stood their ground,
They wanted a change and a new voice had to be found.

Written off over the years,
York exists through hard work, blood, sweat and tears.
I see its love, care and dedication,
I look in the crowd that is what I see in you.

Lessons have been learned,
What we have achieved is what we have earned.
Founded in 67, York we celebrate your 50 years,
Strength, discipline, hard work and winners,
That is why you have bettered your peers.
York opens the heart and minds,
It challenges you to be the best you can be.
York is a place for abundant pride,
Never a soft place or an easy ride.

York was founded on a dream to last,
How quickly fifty years have passed.
York has been a leader and has never followed,
Its excellence, organization and diversity have not mellowed.

Past students who have flown the nest,
Return to push you to achieve your very best.
We challenge everyone to pass the clouds and reach the moon,
That is why with hard work, success never comes too soon.
Although striving to be bigger and better,
It's small enough for individual care.
That is our golden letter.

YORK

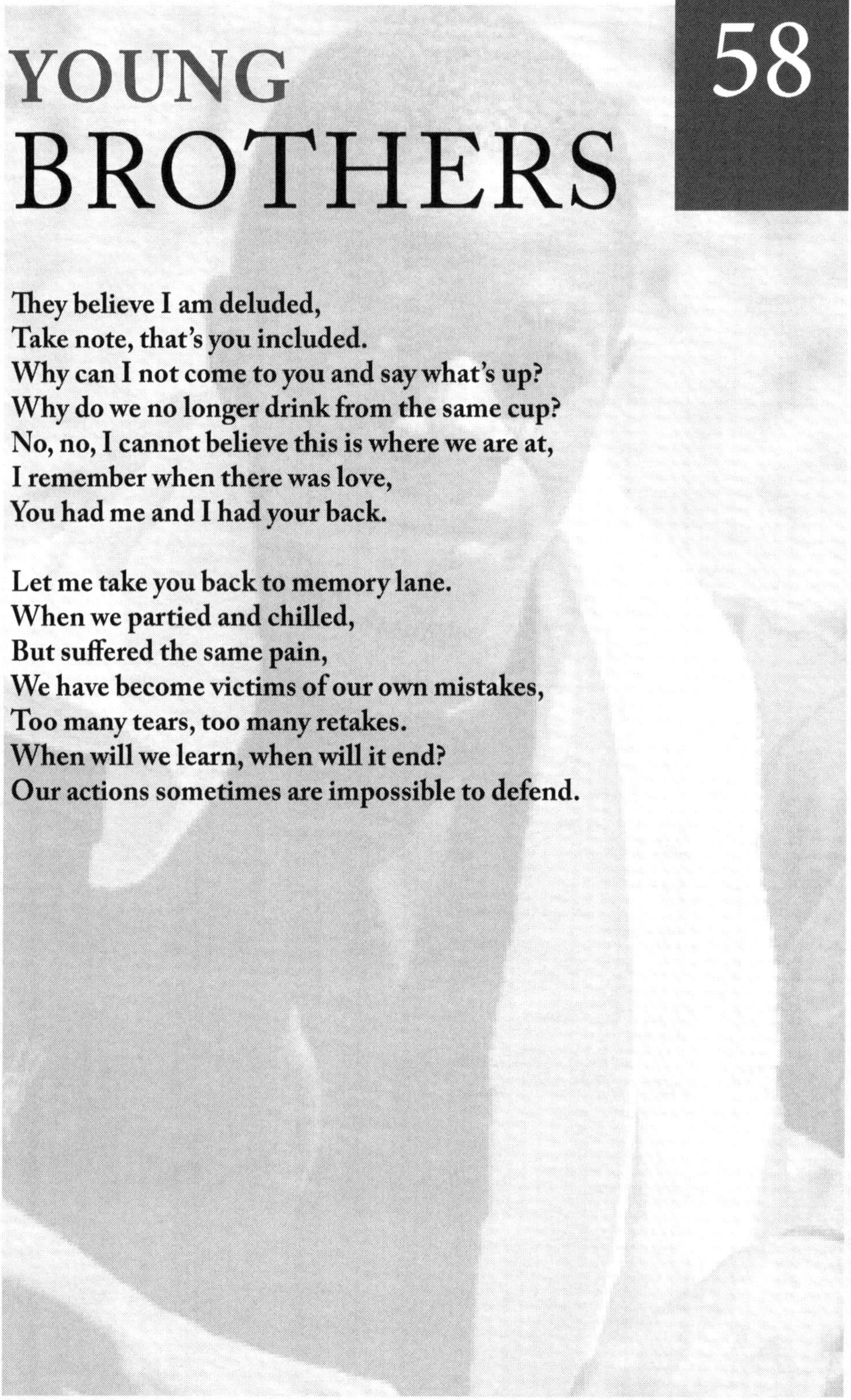

58

YOUNG BROTHERS

They believe I am deluded,
Take note, that's you included.
Why can I not come to you and say what's up?
Why do we no longer drink from the same cup?
No, no, I cannot believe this is where we are at,
I remember when there was love,
You had me and I had your back.

Let me take you back to memory lane.
When we partied and chilled,
But suffered the same pain,
We have become victims of our own mistakes,
Too many tears, too many retakes.
When will we learn, when will it end?
Our actions sometimes are impossible to defend.

YOUNG BROTHERS

Young brothers, listen to a wiser head,
Learn to know when to show grace,
You do understand what I see in you,
Learn your lineage,
To see your future you must know your past.
We are kings,
Now I see daily papers report another death of you,
Do not let your blindness keep you down,
Hold your head high see how much we have grown.
Don't allow social media to tear us apart,
Remember, for us, these people have no love in their heart.

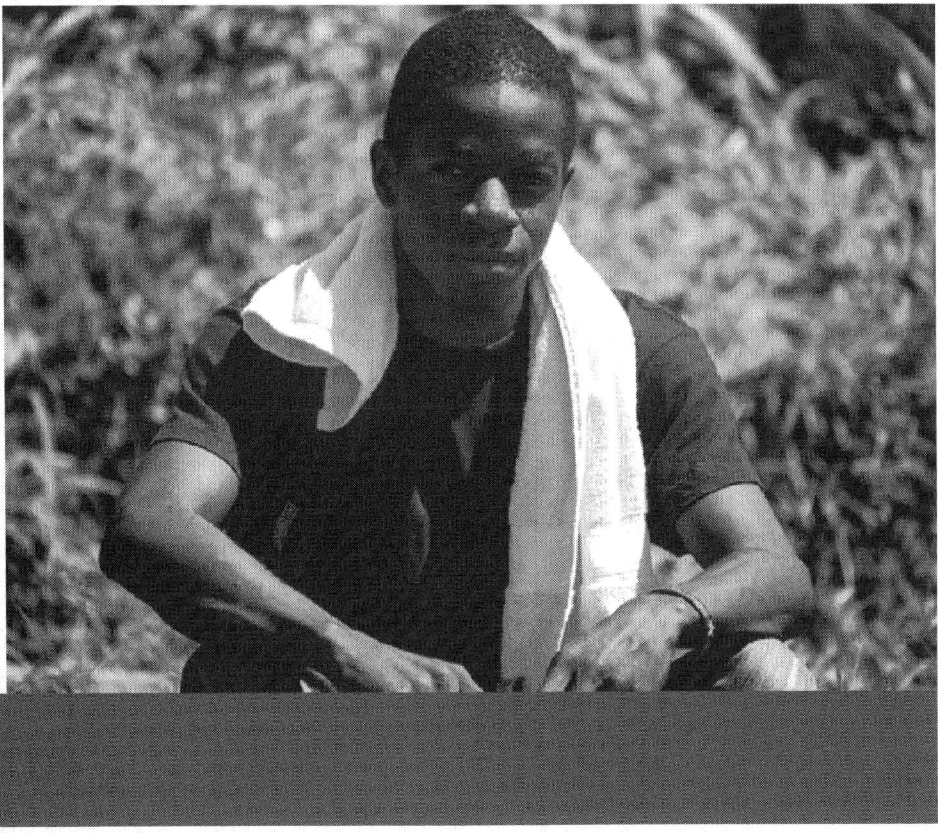

I STRUGGLE WITH WORDS

I struggle with words to say
I love you.
I am sorry for all the hurt I have caused.
I miss you,
I see the beauty in your face.
I wish I knew what you were thinking.

I struggle with words to say,
I know I would never love anyone as I love you,
I am a better man now than the one you left,
My pride is my biggest asset but my worst downfall.

I struggle with words to say,
You make me feel like my legs are taken away.
I am sorry for not being able to say how I miss my family.
For me, this is worse than you can imagine.

I struggle with words to say,
I never meant to hurt you.
Somewhere between stupidity and foolishness, I got lost.
I want to put my arms around you and hold you.
I will always love you!

I struggle with words to say,
I miss your silly jokes.
Many of your thoughts of me are wrong.
I want you to know how I truly feel,
I struggle with words to say
I love you!

I STRUGGLE WITH WORDS

MY WISH

Like a beautiful bird, trapped in a cage,
That book you look at,
But never get past the first page.
I pray for the time when love will dominate,
Our future children will see no more war, no more hate.
So many things in life of which I am unsure,
This is for the people who want to love some more.
Rules are meant to be broken,
Thoughts are meant to be spoken.

Let me try to think, let me speculate,
What would happen, if, for one day we could forget hate?
You wouldn't believe the world we are living in,
So many promises made, but they are only wafer thin.
I do not see me, I see us,
Let's make some noise and create some fuss.
Let's forget who is yellow, brown, white and who is black,
I think as a people we are bigger than that!

The world is ready for change and it is in our hands,
Dismiss all these leaders and their commands.
There should be no oceans running in mothers' eyes,
There should be no bombs dropping,
Breeding so many flies.
I am willing to learn, just like you,
I am new to this,
In an ocean far away,
Let's imagine children playing and getting a goodnight's kiss
Some people need to be heard, they need to be applauded
Now is not the time to be quiet, not to be secretly lauded.

MY WISH

MY RULES

As we get older,
Our thoughts are no longer imprisoned,
We get bolder.

I think of all things in my life I have achieved,
Tricked into ideas when I was young that I believed,
School times educated by semi-educated fools,
Had to survive so I made my own rules.

I have done champagne sipping, late nights and nice cars,
Attended weekend gatherings with low cut dresses and booty bars.

With money at times, I had to be thrifty,
Cooked a meal for nothing had to be nifty.
Now anything I desire, I see it as affordable,
I get it because I deserve it and I am adorable.

Nothing to me is impossible,
Everything I dream is possible.
My dreams my thoughts have not been frozen,
I have lived my life much as I would have chosen.

Lived with love and achieved my laughter lines,
Shed all my baggage and left my grief behind.
Lived my life and banished sedentary,
I will slow down when I get to my century.
My boldness carries me to what I say and do,
As well as each morning I look in the mirror and say,
Welcome to my world, you wonderful you!

MY RULES

MY PILLOW IS MY FRIEND

When love was a canter,
We'd laugh and we would banter.
My broken heart you chose to deceive,
No more wearing my heart on my sleeve.
Did I get lost in a world of fake believe?
So many tears they crystalize in my dreams.

When every song was our song,
In my heart you could do no wrong,
The gentle sway of your curvaceous hips,
The sensuous feel of your fingertips,
Your ample charms,
My eyes did linger,
My heart did charm.

You became the eighth wonder of my world,
To bless me with a boy or a girl,
Beneath my heavy sigh,
My body trembles, it cannot lie.
Just the want of you does not apply,
Standing close to you gravity I do defy.

My heart I can no longer hide,
Your presence alone filled me with awesome pride.
Take my hands and be mine tonight,
This love alone will make the blind see light.
Your beauty so rare,
In the foggiest night,
You stand so clear.

MY PILLOW IS MY FRIEND

Where others brought similarity,
To my life, you brought so much clarity,
So much pain,
No more shame,
My pillow is my friend,
It knows how much I grieve,
So many tears,
They crystalize in my dreams.

My nights I no longer fear,
Now I bless each moment your face appears.
The love you left behind,
In a thousand, only one will find.
Your silly smile and your playful touch,
Now you are gone, they mean so much.

I love you more than yesterday,
Even now in my heart,
I knew you would not stay.
I dream, think and wonder of you,
When you left,
You did what you had to do,
So when the lights are bright,
They will see no tears in sight,
My pillow is my friend,
It knows how much I grieve,
So many tears, they crystalize in my dreams.

LET IT RAIN

Let it rain,
Let it rain,
Let it rain,
Let the rain wash my fears, my tears, and
All my cares away.
For your love how long, I fasted,
Honeymoon over,
One hundred and sixty five days that is how long it lasted.
I promised to loved you as long as my blood flows,
A thousand miles,
I would have walked for you on bare toes.
The sleepless nights,
The unfair fights.
I no longer felt admired
My love for you simply retired

You made me forget who I am,
In truth, you did not give a damn.
A decision that you have just made,
We've just made love,
But, I feel I've only been laid.
Won't be rushing to do this again
I feel so used, so much pain.
Too many compilations of hurtful deeds.
Your selfish wish to see me in pain, to satisfy your needs.
A broken promise made every day,
If it were not for my children, I would have walked away.

Let it rain,
Let it rain,
Let it rain,
Let the rain wash my fears, my tears, and all my cares away.

LET IT RAIN

Over the years I have grown,
Determination and spirit I have shown.
My children and I will stand side by side,
Nothing to be ashamed of, nothing to hide.

No more bouncing off walls on doctors pills,
My life is moving forward not standing still.
Father, I ask no forgiveness for what has been done,
You were there when it started, when all the hurt began.
I feel no remorse,
It is simply nature taking its course.

I think the scars are healing now,
To myself, I have made a vow.
Kiss the rain and
felt your pain.

No more sanctuary in my bedroom walls,
No more using my eyes as waterfalls.
To see my children, how they have grown,
I will be the best father this world has ever known.
Let it rain
Let it rain
Let the rain wash my fears, my tears, and all my cares away

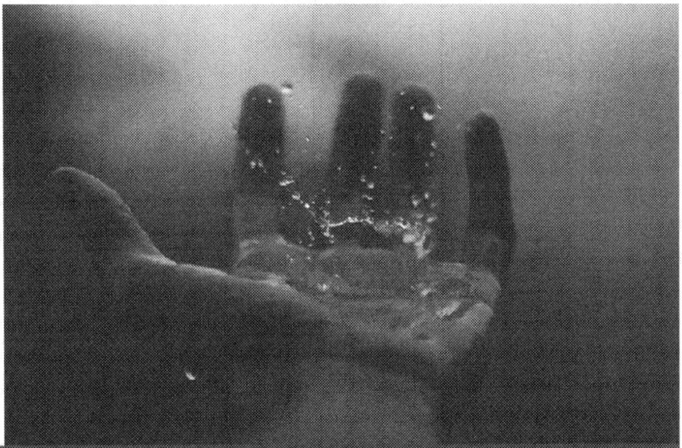

META

I wish I wouldn't repeat, repeat, repeat myself,
I wish I wouldn't repeat, repeat, repeat, repeat myself.

In brief moments of lucidity,
I do not recognize the person that has become me,
Yesterday, I saw my husband for sure,
But my family tells he has been dead for ten years or more.

In moments of despair, desperation,
Frustration, loneliness, sadness anger and pain,
I look to the sky and I call out your name.
I wish I wouldn't repeat, repeat, repeat, repeat myself
I wish I wouldn't repeat, repeat, repeat, repeat myself.

I was once a mother and a wife,
An East End girl so full of life.
Now my days are long and my nights are cold,
There is not much fun in this getting old.
My future once bright, now lies so unsecured,
There is no hope of being cured.

I wish I wouldn't repeat, repeat, repeat, repeat myself,
I wish I wouldn't repeat, repeat, repeat, repeat myself.

No longer allowed out by myself,
Must be accompanied by someone else.
So many new faces, strangers knocking at my door,
I can't remember if I am rich or poor,
But I can remember nineteen forty-four.
The tablets I take, help them to sleep better at nights.
Some things I say, some take for slight.
It is bingo night at the Gala View, and
I am sitting here, simply trying to remember what to do,

I wish I wouldn't repeat, repeat, repeat, repeat myself
Yes, I wish I wouldn't repeat, repeat, repeat, repeat myself.

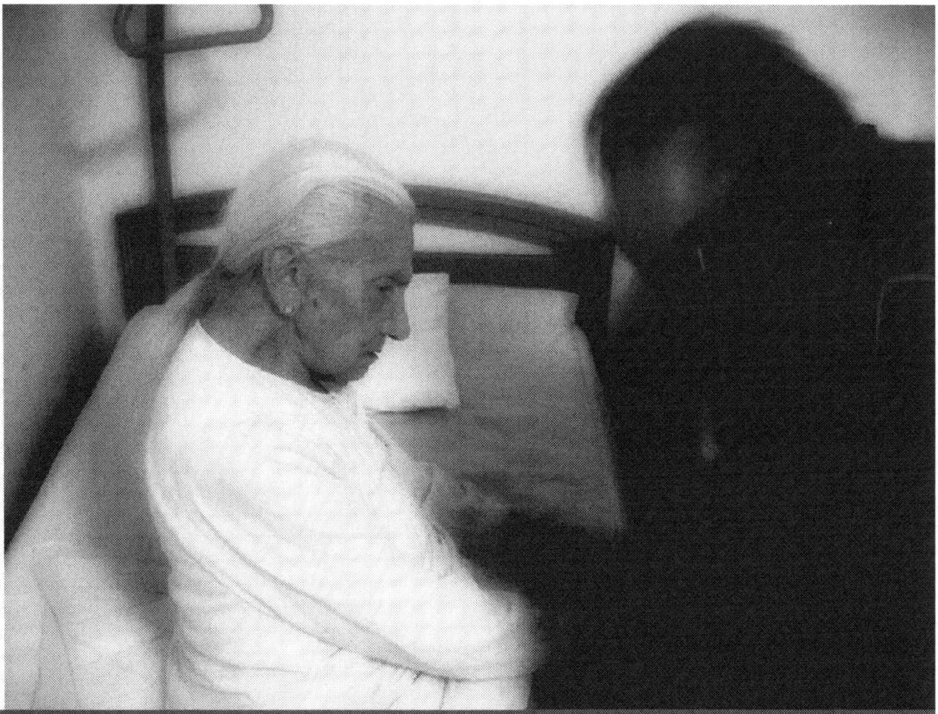

MY PRIDE

My pride is my biggest handicap!
It prevented me from seeing things clearly,
But without it, when I was down,
I would have stayed down.
The days when I felt as if my legs were shackled,
With arms locked behind my back,
When I felt like a blind crab in a maze going nowhere,
I needed you to show faith in me,
Not for you to say that you did not understand me,
Because I did not understand myself,
But I needed your help.

I now realise I needed to grow,
To become the man I am today.
I had to unravel my mind to make my own decisions.
I guess together we were not strong enough,
I felt the pain and the strain but they made me grow,
I guess it is true, there is no I in we,
I knew I needed to find the better part of me.

Although I strive for some kind of perfection,
I recognise I am at least two lifetimes away from that goal.
I wish you had taken me for all my imperfections,
My pride is my biggest handicap!
It prevented me from seeing things clearly,
But without it, when I was down,
I would have stayed down.

MY PRIDE

PART 3

THE BEAUTY OF LOVE

FOOL MYSELF

I know I can fool no one else,
So I'll dream about you and fool myself.

For your love I'm prepared to wait,
My mother told me,
As long as you have hope, you will have faith.
Take me back; give me one more chance,
Allow us to have one more dance.

Please don't leave my heart floating,
You are the love that has my heart voting.
I have been standing waiting in line,
You have tried other loves, why don't you try mine?

I will always keep your memory sacred,
To please me every time you see me,
You don't have to get naked,
I don't want a failure on my heart,
I want nothing to keep us apart.

I know I can fool no one else,
So I'll dream about you and fool myself
Even though life isn't always sunshine and rain,
Forty winks and I'm up ready to love you again.
Memories of you floating around in my head
Your smile, your charm,
I guess I am easily led,
Without trying, you have captured my heart.

FOOL MYSELF

Let no mountain, valley or ocean keep us apart,
In a world famed for fortune and fame,
My life without you is not the same.

Everything I do now has a purpose,
I don't just think about me, I think about us.
At times I may get emotional,
But you can have my body and my soul,
You can have it all.
I want to bring the sunshine to your face,
Let the moon copy your smile,
See your spirits float with the highest clouds.

You satisfy my soul
You quench thirst, you make me whole
Loving you is not a ritual
For me it's more spiritual.

I'm thinking of the times to make little me and you,
That's why I'm here waiting for the chance, give me the queue
I know I can fool no one else,
So I'll dream about you and fool myself.

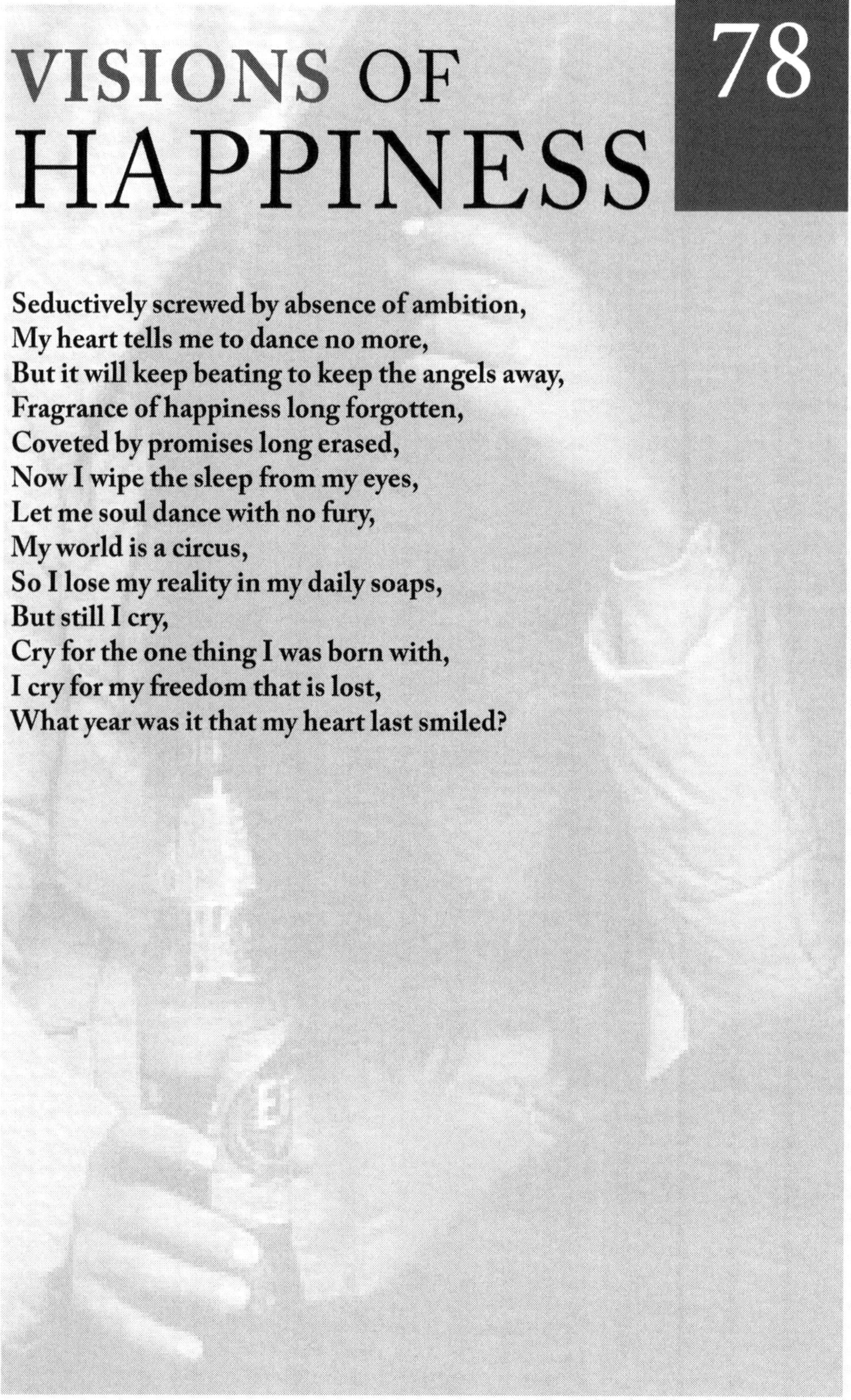

78

VISIONS OF HAPPINESS

Seductively screwed by absence of ambition,
My heart tells me to dance no more,
But it will keep beating to keep the angels away,
Fragrance of happiness long forgotten,
Coveted by promises long erased,
Now I wipe the sleep from my eyes,
Let me soul dance with no fury,
My world is a circus,
So I lose my reality in my daily soaps,
But still I cry,
Cry for the one thing I was born with,
I cry for my freedom that is lost,
What year was it that my heart last smiled?

VISIONS OF HAPPINESS

MY CHILDREN

I watched you stumble and watched you fall,
I watched you grow and I watched you tall.
I watched you learn things I will never know,
I watched you play fight in the sunlight snow.
Cherish, care and love your mother,
For in this life you will never get another.

Don't be lost between greed and ruin,
Because the day of judgement always comes too soon.
People and things will sometimes get you down,
Never let the world see you wear a frown.
Welcome to the world full of tricksters and fools,
For each day, they present new hidden rules.

MY CHILDREN

Welcome to the world where love has been lost,
Where there is mistrust between sisters and brothers,
Welcome to the world of absent fathers,
Lost children and single struggling mothers.
Don't judge a man by the paper he reads,
Judge him by the simple action of his deeds,
Take time to learn and love yourself,
Without that love,
You will never learn to love someone else.

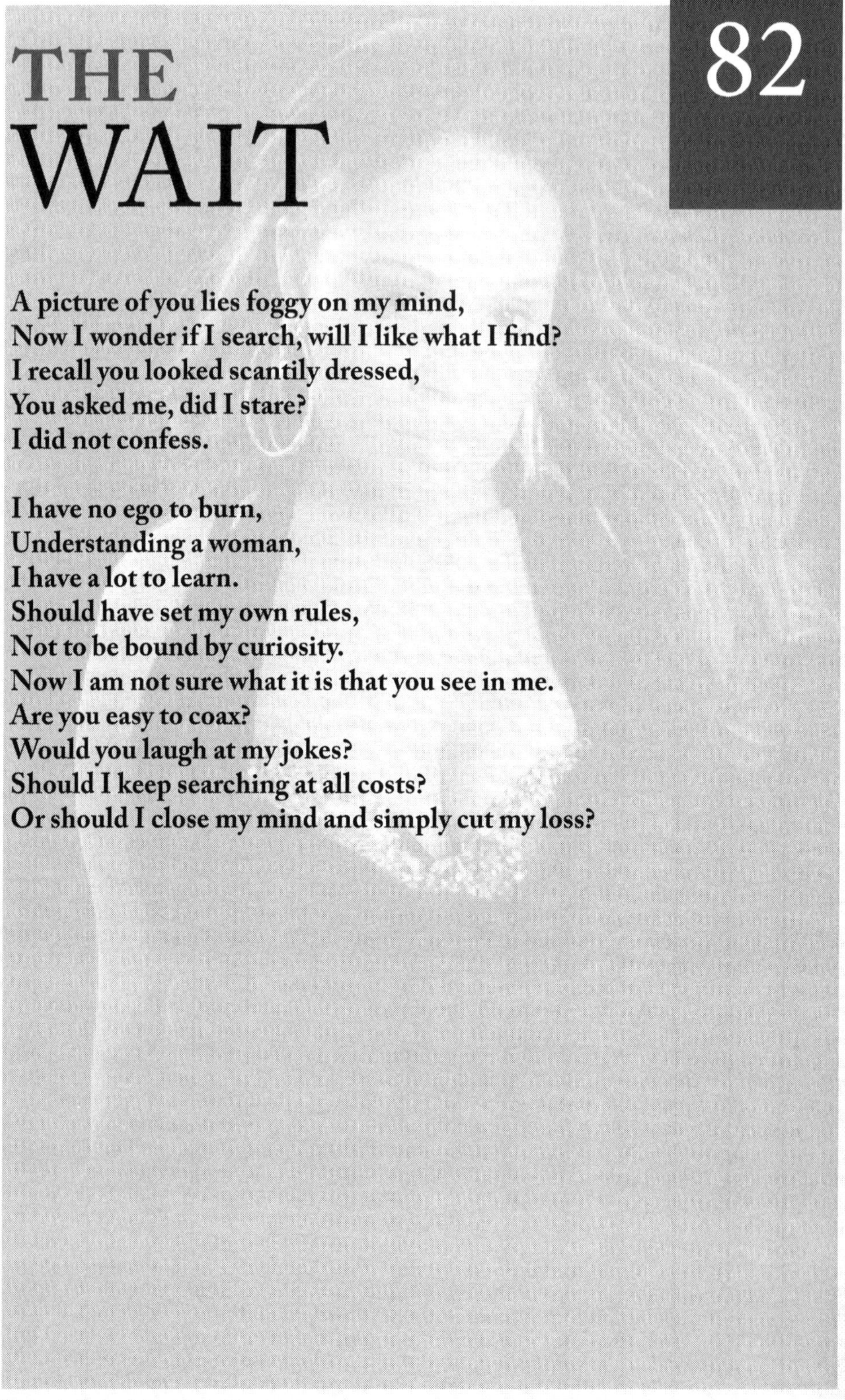

THE WAIT

A picture of you lies foggy on my mind,
Now I wonder if I search, will I like what I find?
I recall you looked scantily dressed,
You asked me, did I stare?
I did not confess.

I have no ego to burn,
Understanding a woman,
I have a lot to learn.
Should have set my own rules,
Not to be bound by curiosity.
Now I am not sure what it is that you see in me.
Are you easy to coax?
Would you laugh at my jokes?
Should I keep searching at all costs?
Or should I close my mind and simply cut my loss?

You dance with a silhouette trailing behind you
All the fellas in line two by two
On that night, what was that perfume you wore?
If we happen to date, would you give me a kind score?

I could be the perfect lover for you,
You will never know if you keep doing what you do.
Stranger things have happened in the past,
Just one date that is all I ask.

THE WAIT

ADDICTION

I find you an orgy of extremism,
A love that borders on the edge of impossibility,
I see in you sometimes a silent pain,
When you are happy,
I see a joy that overflows the widest river.

Why does your shadow not walk beside you?
You crave attention then you reject help.

I am still learning about you,
You have me confused with your translucent thoughts.

I am not sure if I am crazy or accidentally stupid,
When you smile you take my burdens away,
I trip when I walk but for you I still try to run,
How can I make you see that I am trying my best?

The shadows that follow you,
Are now calling my name,
We can't help each other,
If we end up the same.
Your daily prescriptions are really just a token
They won't fix the problems,
It's our minds that are broken

My love for you has no boundaries,
It's yours forever, its perpetual.
I want to be the owner of your last teardrop
Let tomorrow be the new dawn
Yours forever and ever.

ADDICTION

YOUR BEAUTY

Every chartered line on your face tells a story,
Your radiance is like that song with a rift,
It is memorable it is repeated many times over,
You remind me of a wave that has swept everything before it.
I see you in my dreams, in my thoughts,
Your alluring eyes still takes my breath away,
I constantly see that smile,
The one that I tell you looks like a half moon,
The sprinkled gray that you tried to hide,
Captures how beautiful you are.

Your high cheekbones gifted at birth,
Play a role in enveloping my heart,
Even when you sleep, you are a reflection of beauty.
If I look deeply I see that laughter line,
The one you look at in the mirror and touch.

The low lighting by your side cannot hide your beauty,
I have been in a trance since the first day we met.
You inspire days in me you cannot imagine.

The vision of you sitting across the table from me,
Simple though as it maybe,
The moment never slips from my thoughts,
I hold you to account for all the love that is in me.

YOUR BEAUTY

LOVE IS

Love is perfection but it is not perfect,
Love can be senseless but is relentless.
Love is challenging,
Love is growing patience,
Love can be shy, crazy, and spontaneous.
Love can be strong,
Love can be bold,
True love cannot be bought or sold.

Love is audible, forgiving, visual and kind,
Love is not seeking to be fable,
Love is doing because one is able.
Love can sometimes hurt like hell,
Love does not play by rules,
Love turns the cleverest into fools.
Love can take you to the bottomless pit,
Love gives you hope to make you never quit.
Love is there when you feel all hope is lost.
I stand here tonight to thank you (for your love).

Love is strong,
Love is entertaining,
Love is that feeling for that special one,
Love is outlandish; it is out of the ordinary,
Love is freedom of expressions and emotions,
It is contagious, it makes you unable to eat or sleep.
Its non-gender, non-barring colour or size,
Love is holding hands, touching, kissing,
Love is that memory of a captured smile.

Love is dancing, and finger popping,
Love is holidaying and island hopping.
Love is for the romantics, it's written in the stars,
Love is for the late night sippers at cocktail bars.
Love is insatiable,
Love is free spirited and wild at heart.
Love can make the ordinary look great,
Love is found in the old,
Love can be seen in the young,
Love is uncovered in that classic old song,
Love is felt in the perfectionist for details.
Love is in shopaholics for retails.

LOVE IS

THE BEAUTY OF YOU

Let me choose my words so there can be no doubt,
These thoughts are from my heart and totally unscripted.
I am aware how enchanting you are and why they stop and stare,
You are the end of the rainbow I have been chasing all of my life.

My life would be purposeless without you,
Without the love you give.
You are the light and the sun in my universe,
Every day with you is like a thirst day,
Never have enough of you to quench this want.

You have captured my heart,
Wetted my hunger, inflamed my passion
Evoked blazing dreams
Now I believe in déjà vu,
Someone's loss has made my life complete.
You are the dream that I envisioned day and night,
Your love has made me whole.
Fears are no longer attached to my heart,
Let me love you,
With this body to you, I surrender.

Together we will get lost in a passion of life,
Live each day like a borrowed tomorrow,
Embrace the joy life has given to us,
Let us make our own history,
Live, love, laugh and make our dreams come true.
I bless the day my eyes fell on you.

THE BEAUTY OF YOU

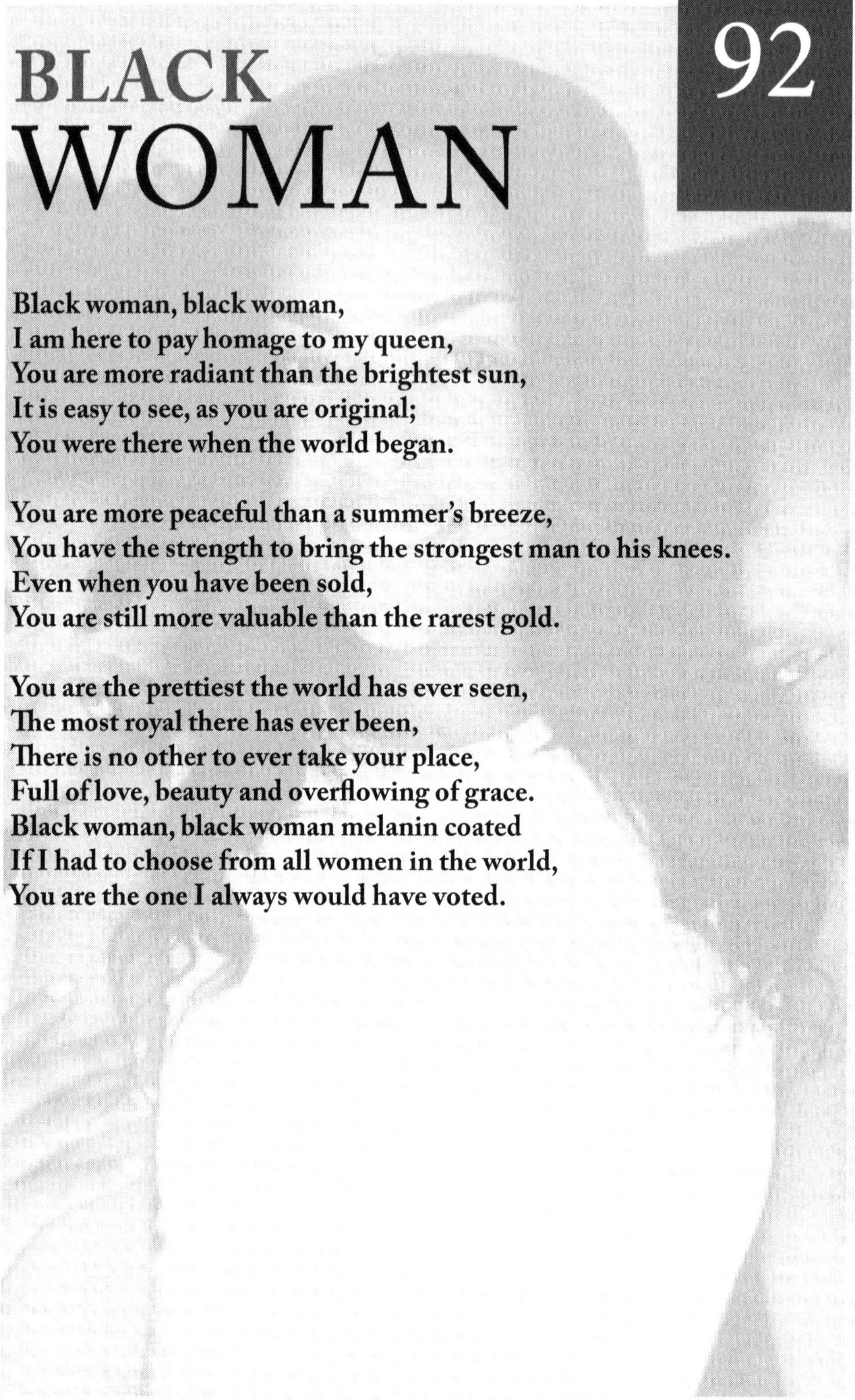

BLACK WOMAN

Black woman, black woman,
I am here to pay homage to my queen,
You are more radiant than the brightest sun,
It is easy to see, as you are original;
You were there when the world began.

You are more peaceful than a summer's breeze,
You have the strength to bring the strongest man to his knees.
Even when you have been sold,
You are still more valuable than the rarest gold.

You are the prettiest the world has ever seen,
The most royal there has ever been,
There is no other to ever take your place,
Full of love, beauty and overflowing of grace.
Black woman, black woman melanin coated
If I had to choose from all women in the world,
You are the one I always would have voted.

When my spirit was broken
You came to my rescue and made sure it was lifted,
Your love is stronger than the strongest bond,
But your tongue is sharper than the sharpest knife.

Black woman, black woman
From sugarcoated to dark rum complexion,
You have made me grow and I love our unique connection,
Black woman, black woman many have tried,
But it's impossible to compare.
Black woman, black woman
I stand and admire the beauty that you hold so rare.

BLACK
WOMAN

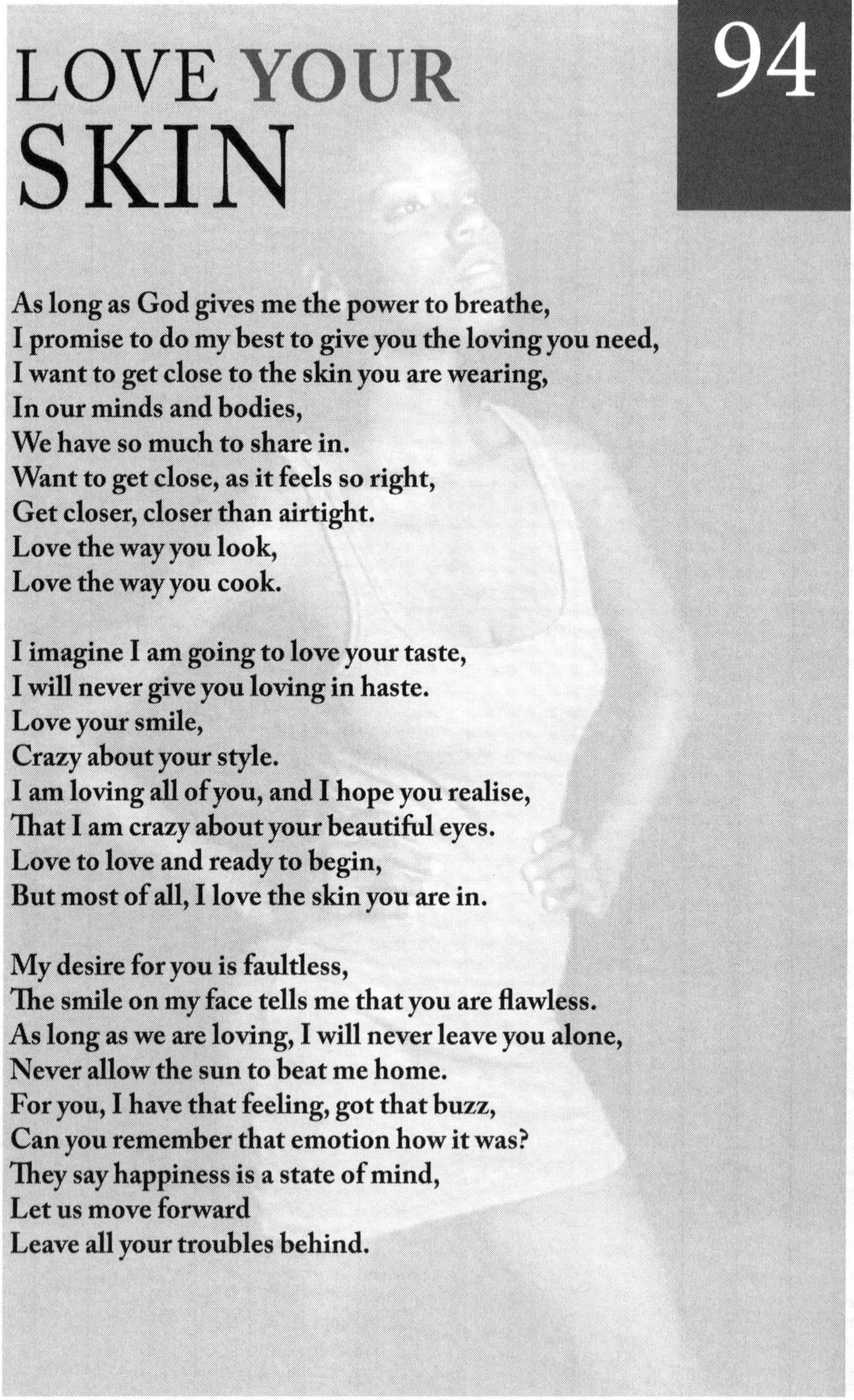

94

LOVE YOUR SKIN

As long as God gives me the power to breathe,
I promise to do my best to give you the loving you need,
I want to get close to the skin you are wearing,
In our minds and bodies,
We have so much to share in.
Want to get close, as it feels so right,
Get closer, closer than airtight.
Love the way you look,
Love the way you cook.

I imagine I am going to love your taste,
I will never give you loving in haste.
Love your smile,
Crazy about your style.
I am loving all of you, and I hope you realise,
That I am crazy about your beautiful eyes.
Love to love and ready to begin,
But most of all, I love the skin you are in.

My desire for you is faultless,
The smile on my face tells me that you are flawless.
As long as we are loving, I will never leave you alone,
Never allow the sun to beat me home.
For you, I have that feeling, got that buzz,
Can you remember that emotion how it was?
They say happiness is a state of mind,
Let us move forward
Leave all your troubles behind.

Now let us do something clever,
Let's put your heart back together.
First thing to do from the start,
Remove all the pain from your heart.
First time I saw you time lapsed,
Only woke when my heart gasped.
The likelihood that we fall in love.
Is like the hand in the perfect glove.
Love to love and ready to begin,
Most of all, love the skin you are in.

LOVE YOUR SKIN

SPOTLIGHT TO YOUR HEART

Had a thought,
Closed my eyes,
Turn the tables of my life,
Spotlight to your heart baby.

She walked into the room and created a stir,
Every man wishing he were with her.
See this woman is honey and spice made,
She is love made, not street made, she is home made.

I am talking about my insecurities,
Life is full of many uncertainties.
First time I saw her, all I could say was wow!
Thought to myself, I need to call my minister now.
I think I am ready to make that vow,
Even if I can't explain this reason or how.
I want to be the itch in your bone,
Be the number one, number in your phone.

For my responsibilities,
You will never catch me shirking.
For your love, I will always keep working.
To you, I will always be kind,
You are someone special, one of a kind.
With you, I have forgotten to use my senses,
Forgotten what common sense is.
If I could use a magic wand,
The wish would be for you to accept my hand.
This feeling is so real, so strong,
About your body, I could write the perfect song.
I am not just thinking about my loins,
But somewhere between where my soul and my heart joins.

SPOTLIGHT TO YOUR HEART

We could do things together, others won't mention,
You can dream about them when you're drawing your pension.
Lady, I want to make you feel comfortable,
Whenever you feel, you can come to me.
Take you somewhere out of your reach,
Somewhere close to Daytona Beach.
But baby, keep your clothes on,
Let me use my imagination.
You may not get another glance,
Life is about taking a chance.
Forget consequences,
If you do not,
You may not know what true romance is.

Life is about crossing the road,
Sometimes carrying the heavy load.
When you are old and grey, you can reminisce,
Now you are young picture this!
I do not want to be the stick in the mud,
But if you tell me no,
My eyes will flood.
I love you because
I love you always,
Had a thought,
Close my eyes,
Turn the pages of my life,
Spotlight to your heart, baby.

98

LOVE WITHOUT EXPECTATIONS

Four walls and a silent room,
There was no hello, no goodbye,
No, how was your day?
More thoughts of another night to fake it again,
No questions, did you cry today?
Do not shout at me,
Do not call my name put my name down!

Your world became so distorted,
Then I knew I had to make it.
Can't you see?
All the lessons I have learned,
This fool is not going to love you no more.
When the pain became unbearable,
My love died between each breath that I took.

To my new love I say,
To earn me, you must absorb me,
Break the seal to my heart,
You need to capture my mind, my soul,
Search for my imagination and my heart,
Then you will find my love and my body.

LOVE WITHOUT EXPECTATIONS

I am me, I have love to give,
I have all my desires.
Ask me questions!
Do not take my love for granted,
Now I have a will to live to love,
Now I live with expectations,
Write my name on your heart,
Capture my soul,
Surpass it if you can,
Use my name with love; use my name with care,
Never put my name down!

BLAME IT ON LOVE

I tried and I failed,
I tried and I failed again,
To get you of out my mind,
Maybe it is your eyes,
It could be the way you smile so openly.
Maybe it's the way you hold my attention without trying,
Or it could be the way I find you so breathtakingly intoxicating,
Your elegance is only matched by your seductive smile,
Do you notice my naked desire for your lips?

Having said that, do not blame me, blame it on love.
Blame it on the fact I would love to kiss you,
Blame it on me seeing you in my bed,
Blame it on me wanting to love you,
Blame it on me wanting to give you all my love,
Blame it on you loving me back,
Blame it on my want for you,
Most of all, blame it on love!

You may say my eyes are blurred,
But something in my body you have stirred.
Could it be your warmth or your touch?
My mind is working overtime thinking of you so much,
You're uncomplicated but compelling,
You are wonderful with grace and style,
I see you in my arms; I'm driving you wild,
These words are not endless compliments,
Do not blame me,
Blame it on love.

BLAME IT ON LOVE

MY THOUGHTS AS I AWAKE

102

As I awake from my slumber and draw my first breath,
I am consciously aware that it is less than two weeks since we first met.
I think of you, I feel the need to say something clever,
My thoughts freeze but I wish this feeling will last forever.
I want to take you miles away from your comfort zone,
Put happy thoughts in your head when you're alone,
I know I may make mistakes with you,
But I will learn so next time I will know what to do.

Somehow, with you I allow my thoughts to leak,
I feel it when you smile but do not speak.
I see your face in every blink that I make,
You consume every breath that I take,
You're the smile that could launch a thousand ships,
I want to kiss those beautiful lips.
I am not sure where this story goes,
Could you be my rose and bring this to a perfect close.

MY THOUGHTS AS I AWAKE

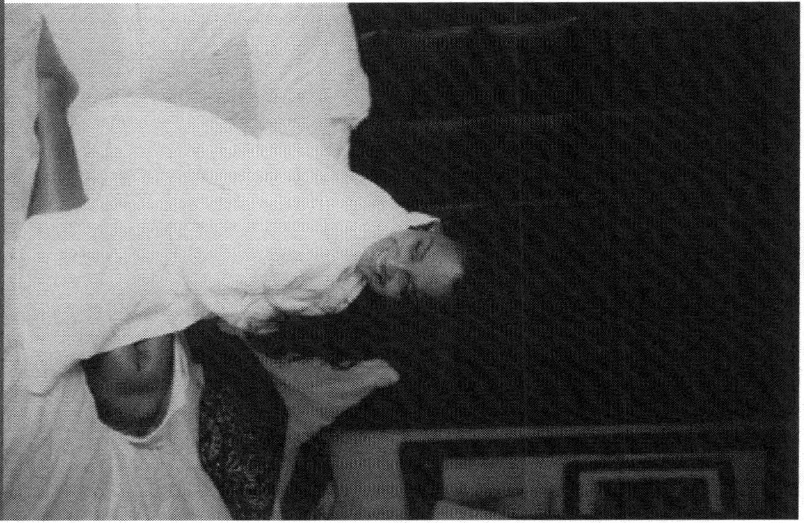

ABOUT YOU

It's funny,
But I feel stronger now that I know that I'm weak,
Give me five minutes of your time and allow me to speak.
You share your thoughts and you think it's a distraction,
But I think it's a reaction from a timeless attraction.

When I look at you,
I forget what I'm about to say,
I want to love you and take your breath away,
I'm not perfect,
But if you get to know me,
I think I'm worth it.

There is a spark between us,
I don't care who else knows.
We have so much in common,
Let's see where the wind blows.
So many things about you that hold my attention,
Your beauty, your charm, just a few to mention.

ABOUT YOU

Love that you don't play by the book,
You've captured my heart with just one look.
You're the one thought that occupies my mind,
Just give me a clue, if you want to be mine.

I could love you like you've never been loved before,
The kind of love that keeps coming back for more.
Dismiss those inhibitions and that fruitless pride,
These feelings that are rising are impossible to hide.
It's like a tsunami or when two oceans collide,
It's coming from way deep inside.
Love and live life to the most,
And for your body let me be the perfect host.

YOUR WORTH

I know today, to me you may feel so distant,
To hate me there may be no resistance.
You may find it hard to recover,
I hope tomorrow a rainbow you will discover.
Unsure if there is anything I could ever do,
To get back into you.
I am making an admission,
I made a bad decision.

We have our flaws
But I hope your pain eventually thaws.
I've made mistakes but I will learn to love you more,
If you do not see it, it is because you have closed your door.

I was caught between stupidity, ego, pride and lies,
I see the heartache I've caused, I was not that wise,
We may have our ups and downs,
But I promise, I will never use your name with a frown.
The fact that we have made it this far,
Shows what a special person you are.
You are the most beautiful woman on earth
Any man loving you would know your true worth.

YOUR WORTH

YOURS

I want to be your poster boy,
Let me be the one to bring you joy.
Your name, I promise, I will not scandalize,
You mean so much to me, that I hope you realize.

My bad days are in the past,
My love for you is going to last.
Some parts of my life are colourful to paint,
Let me be your rock, I will be your perfect saint.

This kind of love is so incredible and so rare,
We will have so many special moments to share.
You are the only candidate for my heart,
I am going to take my time with you and act smart,
I want to make a life with you,
Do all the things together that lovers do.

You stimulate my mind, body and soul,
With you, I want to grow outrageously old.
You have danced your way into my heart,
This is just the beginning, just the start!

YOURS

You stimulate me and I'm happy to be your clown,
Notice my feelings; see how much they have grown,
For your love I will go the distance go for broke,
There will be stimulating conversations and practical jokes.

I am going to love you more than you've been loved before,
And when my eyes bless each day, I will love you more,
I do not know if I believe in luck or fate
How I feel about you there is no debate.

I have seen you smile with love written on your face,
I have given my heart,
I know it is in a wonderful place.
All my Casanova days are over now,
That is a promise and I will make that vow.
I think of you when you are miles away,
You thrill my mind, soul and body,
I see your face in my dreams,
I know in my heart we belong,
I can feel it, these feelings are so strong.

LAZY DAYS

I see sun kissed rays on your sweet ebony face,
My mind reciting a mental picture,
Eyes lazily closed,
Smile borrowed from a do not forget moment,
These are days of decadence.

I embrace your warmth,
The love that you have brought into my life,
Your uncontrollable passion,
When music is the sound of your voice calling my name,
Then sorrow is the moment that you leave my side,
When you return and I hold you so tight,
I accept now that you will never be mine.

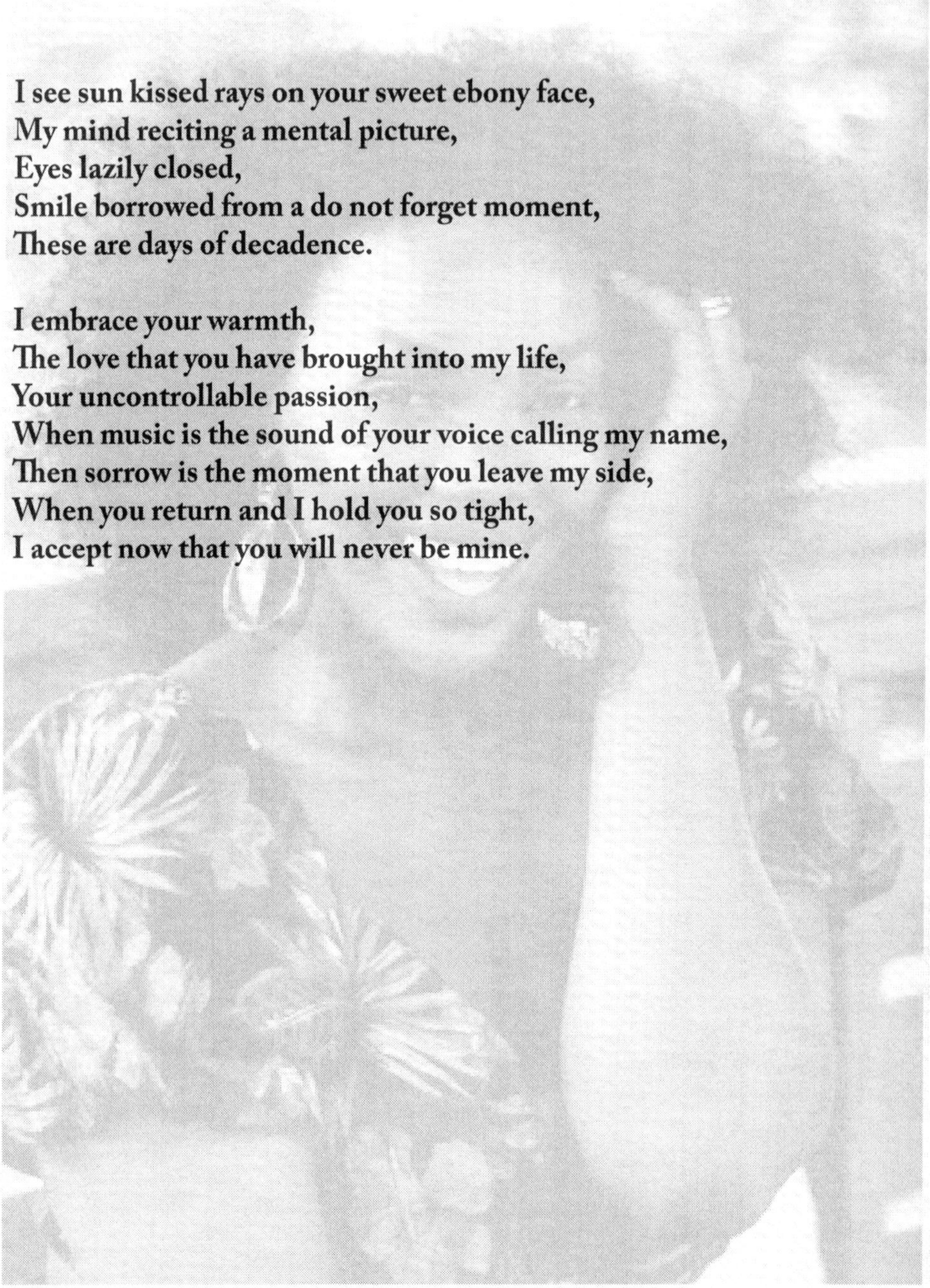

How can something so wrong feel so right with you?
Each day, I cannot help loving you more,
We have feelings that are not covered by laws,
Our bands belong to someone else,
But our hearts will always belong to each other.
We know we are fallible,
Just the same, I want to love you more.

LAZY DAYS

THE BEST LOVE

I dream of late nights and misspent days,
The steamy nights and those faraway gazes.
My thoughts I wish I had spoken,
Now it is too late the spell is broken.
When the day breaks and the sun rises,
I see different people in different guises.
I am not Tom Ford, Armani or Gucci lookalike,
I was just me trying to do what I thought was right,
When you spoke, I suddenly realised how you sounded,
Your sad words hit me, left me completely astounded.

In my darkest days, you are my brightest sunshine,
Without you, I see no future, I can't leave you behind.
Sometimes I look and you ask why I stare,
Because your eyes sometimes strips me bare.
Your smile is my bait,
That is why for your love I am prepared to wait,
8,9,10 times of the year, you drive me mad,
But you are still the best love I have ever had.
The odds against me maybe heavily stacked
Give me a chance to fight and get you back.

THE BEST LOVE

THE BEST OF ME

I may be dumb, act stupid and drive you to despair,
It doesn't mean I'm someone who simply does not care.
Suddenly I do not feel so smart,
I have said something that affected your heart.
To make up, I will do whatever I need to do,
I still have a bucket full of love just for you.

Let my actions not just my words bring you joy,
Just use my body as your favourite toy,
With you, I will not take on more than I can handle,
Won't leave you sitting like an ornament on my mantle.
I am glad we spoke and debated,
You could have taken my number and had it deleted.

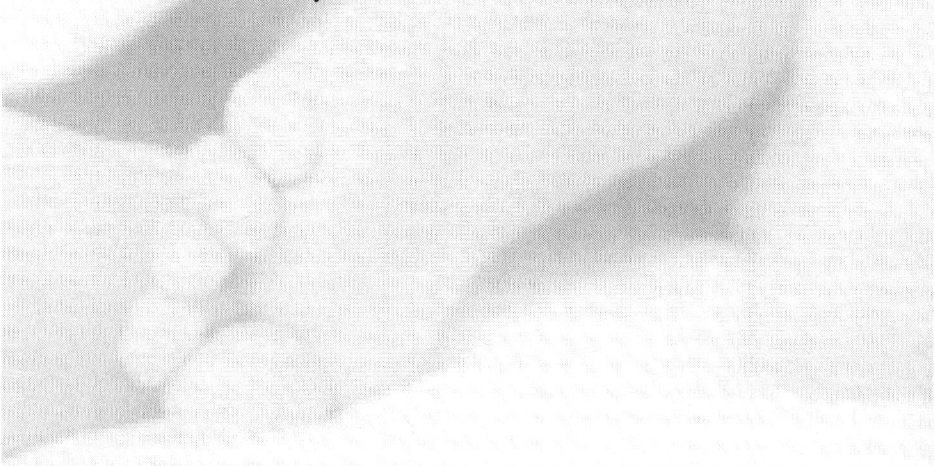

Let us make a promise, to never be separated,
Whatever happens between us will not be ill fated.
You are my future to build my hopes upon,
When I met you, my new life began.
No games, no tricks, our time together will be blessed,
Nothing about me will make you question or second guess.

You are the light that shines different from the rest,
Each day with you, make me my very best.
You are the wish, the dream that has come true,
Together we can be tighter than glue.
Let us put our wrongs to the past.
From this day my love for you is going to last.

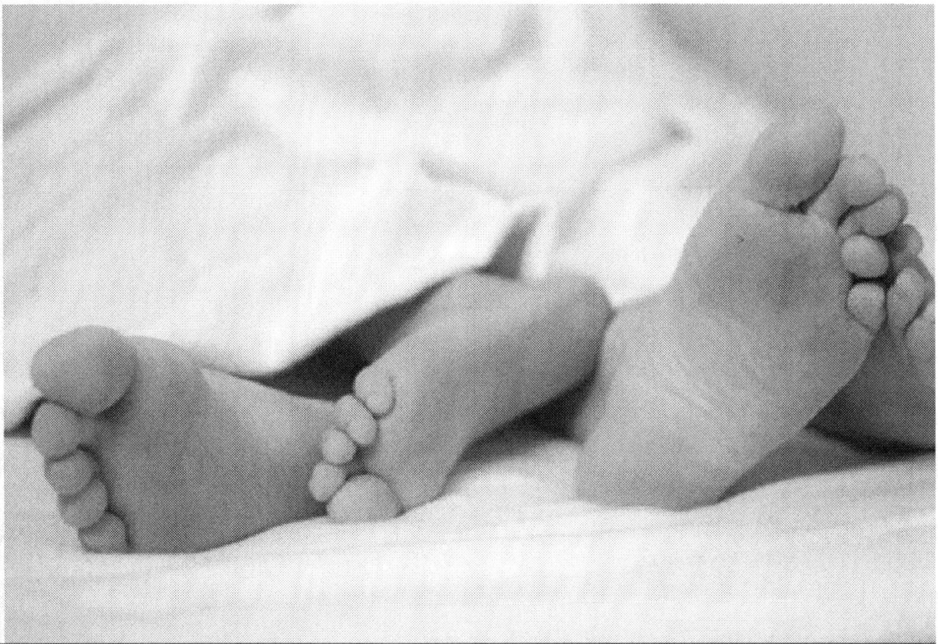

GETTING TO KNOW YOU

Pardon me, do mind if I sit with you, talk with you?
Maybe later even take a walk with you?
Do you like to kiss with your eyes closed?
You look like someone who wears fine clothes.

With a body like yours, I would love to explore,
I could make you love as you never have before.
With these strong arms holding you tight,
Everything would be so perfect, be so right.

I imagine you walking through my bedroom door,
Then giving you so much loving, and so much more.
I have thoughts of you wearing nothing but a smile,
I look and admire your beauty, allure and style.

I have a vision of you smiling in my head,
You are lying naked and you are in my bed,
My kind of loving is not what you call basic,
So do not lose this moment, please do not waste it.

If you ever loved me, you would want me back,
I am fun, loving, thoughtful, and crazy like that.
No need to waste this moment and conversate,
If you do, then tomorrow will be too late.

GETTING TO KNOW YOU

See that smile you are modelling?
Keep it, as tonight we will be cuddling.
Looking at you, I want to kiss your lips
Crazy about those Coca-Cola shaped hips.

Forget all those tears that flowed from your eyes,
From this voice, you will never hear any lies.
When you speak, I hear a melody in your voice,
Take me or leave me for someone that is your choice.

I can see in your pretty brown eyes,
Let's take our loving to memorable highs,
Baby no one is counting, keeping the score,
Still keep coming girl, keep coming back for more.

HOW I SEE YOU

Lying next to you,
I feel the silence of the night as you breathe,
The dim of the light conceals your pretty face,
That little laughter line you touch so often,
Your beauty blows me away.

Last night when we loved and you told me,
"Take me and love me as I am,
These curves of mine belong to time,
But I want you to hold and to admire".
I think of your smile and my heart skips a beat,
Your kisses so sweet,
I watch you in slumber
I am jealous of the soft sheet covering your body.

In the golden stillness, did I hear your heart beat?
Memories come back to my mind of you sighing,
Arms reaching for comfort,
Our bodies displaying magical acts of love,
Lips are tightly locked,
Our bodies entwined
To have and to hold this moment is mine,
Our bodies ached for more,
You pull me close, closer than close,
We become one.
I feel the woman in you,
You feel the hunger in me.
Melanin to melanin we are more than one.

PROMISE

I see you as verbally challenging,
Extraordinarily striking,
Exceptionally thought provoking.

I am praying and hoping that you are somehow into me.
I am not looking for comfort,
I am looking for amazing,
I am not fussed on the title of being your king,
Yet I could see you being my queen.

I would live a life with you where seconds do not count,
When an hour is just a moment,
When a day is an hour,
When a week is just a long day,
We can love, laugh and still have time to pray.

PROMISE

With you in my life, there would be no passenger.
I love that look in your eyes.
You know you have me under your spell,
Without you, I know I would be living in hell.

Something about you has touched my soul,
Hard as I try, it is impossible to control.
I will not make promises that are easy to break,
A beautiful family, you and I could create,
At my worst, I will always put you first,
You have an amazing heart, I claim as mine.
Used all my gifted lives to be with you,
I've used all nine.

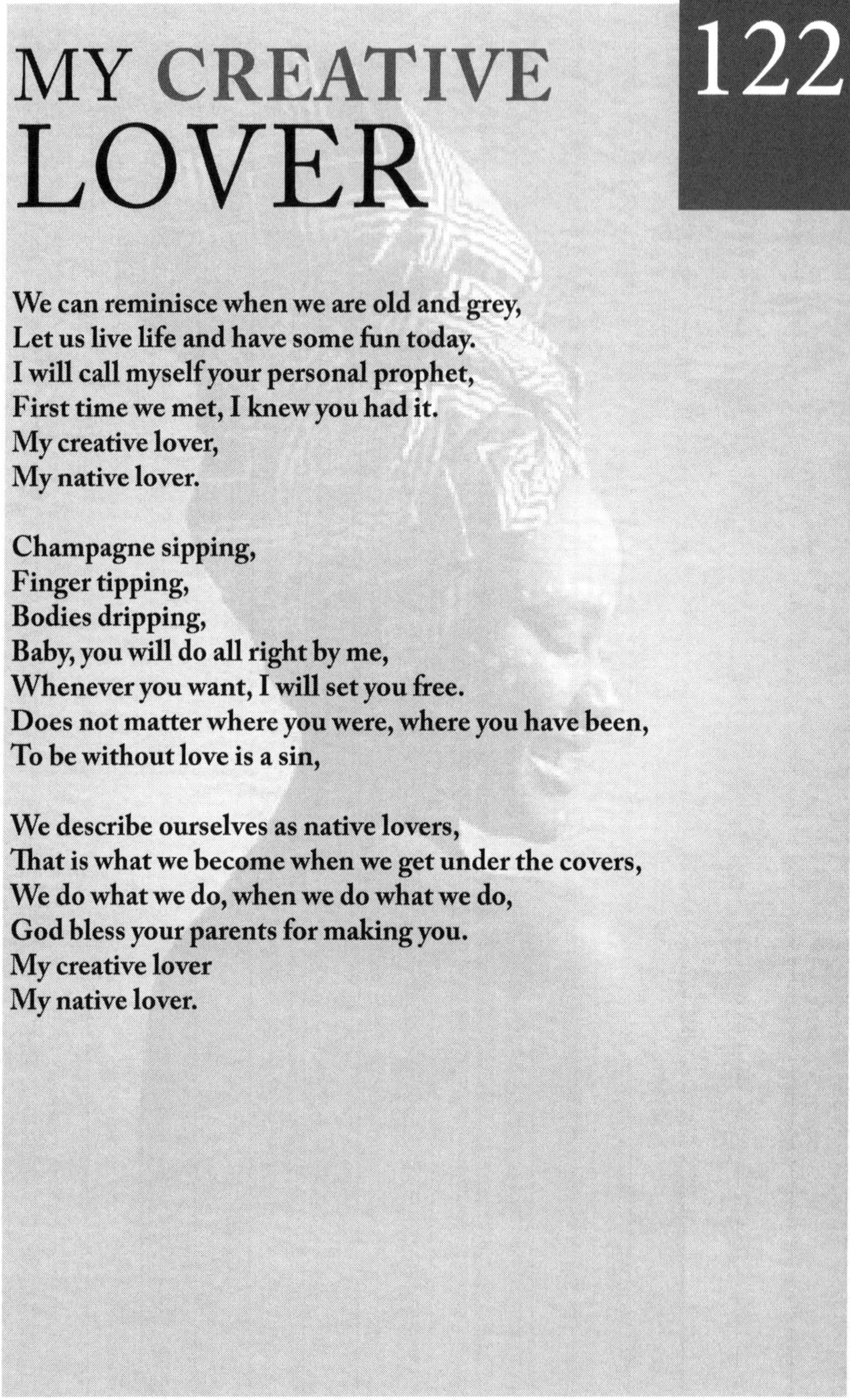

MY CREATIVE LOVER

We can reminisce when we are old and grey,
Let us live life and have some fun today.
I will call myself your personal prophet,
First time we met, I knew you had it.
My creative lover,
My native lover.

Champagne sipping,
Finger tipping,
Bodies dripping,
Baby, you will do all right by me,
Whenever you want, I will set you free.
Does not matter where you were, where you have been,
To be without love is a sin,

We describe ourselves as native lovers,
That is what we become when we get under the covers,
We do what we do, when we do what we do,
God bless your parents for making you.
My creative lover
My native lover.

MY CREATIVE LOVER

TEMPTED

The bands on our hands tells us we have other demands,
So, we jest and flirt,
Damn, you look good in that skirt,
Wish these hands could touch your slender waist,
Yeah I know I have wonderful taste,
I know we are tempted,
Much more of this and my will have relented.

Thoughts of you, thoughts of me, thoughts of us,
You are living in my mind from dawn to dusk.
Imagine if our worlds had never met,
Now imagine a gambler never taken a bet.

You are so flirtatious, outrageous, and contagious.
Thoughts of you, thoughts of me, thoughts of us,
Love the fact that you wear no ego,
Anytime girl you can call me, call me your Don Amigo,
Now I know it is not right, but if you keep smiling,
Rules may be broken and we might just might.

TEMPTED

PASSION OF LOVE

I love love when love has no barrier on colour,
I love love when love has no religion,
I love love when love has no gender,
I love love when love has no thoughts on your waist.

When your face is the thought of the day,
Your impish smile, those cherished lips,
Your unchiseled face filled with a thousand emotions,
Your open heart broken, but not tainted,
Your eyes to me, how they talk,
I am mesmerized by your walk.

I see things in you a thousand eyes will not notice,
Like when you smile, a dimple appears for a second,
Or when we kiss your left eye closes first.
Your soul challenged me to take your breathe away,
So, when we make love, I go over and over and over,
Every inch of your body,
To places that are filled with erotic zones.

I love the mounds, the bumps, the curves,
The woman in you,
Who is not afraid to say
Let us do this my way
And when our bodies are entwined and become one,
With our hearts joined in that passionate emotion,
Then I look and I can see the stars,
But looking closer, I realise it's the love that burns in your eyes,
When our bodies are spent and totally wasted,
With emotions running raw,
I will forever and ever, hold your love deep in my heart.

PASSION OF LOVE

MY VALENTINE

Beauty, elegance, charm and personality,
These are the things that you see in me.
I've made you smile,
That is how it should always be,
Girl when I look at you,
Sometimes you send shivers down my spine,
I pinch myself, I cannot believe that you are really mine.

The days of my empty thoughts,
Have been replaced by the love you have brought,
Mountains are to be climbed,
If I had to climb one every day,
I would never leave you behind.

When all is said, and sometimes written,
I look at you and I am still smitten,
I hope the day never comes,
That I am taking you for granted,
Because you need to know,
You are all I have ever wanted.

Words are said,
Promises sometimes broken,
Yet the spell you have me under
I hope I am never woken.

I am not like the biblical Moses,
I am more champagne and roses,
With you sometimes I confess.
I can be truly unruly,
Despite that,
My heart is always with you, always truly.

MY VALENTINE

TRAPPED

Are you my gift of tomorrow?
Or are you my future pain, misery and sorrow?
Just one thought of you gets me so high,
You make me feel I have the strength of a giant eagle,
But I'm still unable to fly,
When I think of your kisses, your touch and your wishes,
I force myself to draw a breath,
I realise you are not as innocent as the air that you breathe,
I have to admit that I am little naive,
I maybe out of my depth.

Will you be the one who will make me behave?
Or will you be the one who will send me to an early grave?
I see you as my dream and to fulfill my wishes,
But will you leave me with nothing except my dirty dishes?
Will you be my saviour?
Are you the one who will make me change behaviour?

Let me know are you my saviour or are you my curse?
I see passion in you that is impelling and gravitating

Your loving is exceptionally generous, it's absorbing,
It's arousing, stirring, intriguing and exciting.

You arouse thoughts I should not think about,
Your scent is enchanting,
Your kisses are filled with deep suggestions.
Should I string along and take the bait?
Or should I borrow common-sense and learn to wait?
Will you be my saviour or will you be my curse?

TRAPPED

MOTHER'S DAY

Happy Mother's Day, you deserve it
You are class, beauty, gravel and spit,
You are the life and soul of any party to be,
You put a smile on my face, so happy you are with me!
You are inspirational, funny, cute,
Pretty with a wonderful wit.
You are everyone's favourite girl,
His or her number one hit.

The love and care you give is treasured by all,
You stand as a brick everybody's emotional wall.
You are the irreplaceable stone,
The one they can never clone,
If I were to spend a week in mars with someone,
It would be you; I would choose to be with,
I am saying that because you are fun,
Lovable and we make a wonderful hit.

You are more special to me than you will ever know,
You are my yesterday, today and all of my tomorrow.
You are my ball of sunshine,
You are my bright scenic waterfall,
Just knowing your are there fills our hearts.
Happy Mother's Day
We love you so much.

MOTHER'S
DAY

MY MOONFACE

I'm amazed at your strength to learn, your tenacity,
That is one of the reasons why I love you to bits.
You fill your mother and me with so much pride,
You hear it in our voices, it is impossible to hide.

Let far-away lands be no stranger to you,
Take my blessings to do your best in life,
Reach for the sky and never worry if you fail,
FAIL is only first attempt is learning.
Dust yourself off and be ready again,
Tomorrow morning again I'll will try.

Search and develop a passion for life,
The passion will guide you in troubles and strife.
Three years of studying has gone so fast,
Late nights studying, how long will this last?
Diligence, perseverance and enthusiasm,
Have made your dreams come true.
Everyone is so happy, so incredibly proud of you,
Choose something that gives you passion to strive,
I promise you will never work a day in your life.

Hard times will come and hard times will go,
Learn from it, as a person it will make you grow.
Never quit when adversity comes knocking at your door,
Stand strong, head high, smile, and be ready for more.
The sun always shines somewhere on the bleakest day,
So remember to work, rest, pray and play.
I hope life you continues to grow,
You are wonderful, beautiful as you are,
My love for you will never change,
Whether you are close, or if you are an ocean far.

MY MOONFACE

MY LIFE STORY

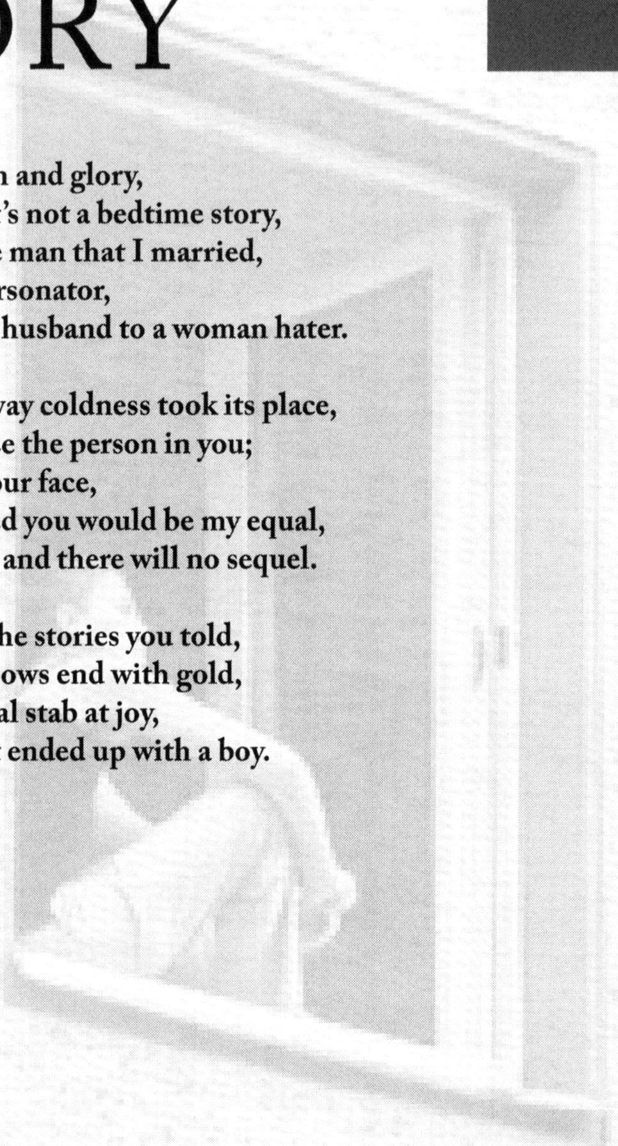

I'm sharing my pain and glory,
It's not beautiful; it's not a bedtime story,
You're not the same man that I married,
All I see is an impersonator,
You've gone from a husband to a woman hater.

When love went away coldness took its place,
No longer recognize the person in you;
I don't recognize your face,
I hoped and I prayed you would be my equal,
But life turned bad and there will no sequel.

No longer believe the stories you told,
Found not all rainbows end with gold,
This was my first real stab at joy,
Married a man, but ended up with a boy.

Someone who was all three, a liar, thief and a cheat,
Couldn't stay in that marriage couldn't stand the heat.
When I realised I was living with an animal,
To survive, wrote myself a manual.
Reflected how I was neglected,
So made a vow and got my heart protected.

It's been rough,
And it's been tough,
But through my struggles and strife,
I am determined to live a better life.
I've finally laid my cards on the table,
It's not been easy, not been pretty,
But at last I am free to live my life,
I feel much more able.

BITTERNESS

Your cold beat-less heart no longer belongs to me,
Your God forgave you,
You have set yourself free.

When we met, for me, it was real it was not a flutter,
Now two years on, you spread like butter.
I gave my all, but you threw it away,
Treated my love as if it was a cheap holiday.
The pain you left when you closed your door,
Nothing I did was enough you always wanted more.

My bitterness I can no longer hide,
I was the stool, the fool you continued to ride,
You stole my heart now hidden away,
On your demise, it will be glorious day.

A fridge now lies where my heart once laid,
I was a fool and cruelly played.
Your desire was so craven,
You used me as your safe haven.
To others, I appear to be sad lonely and twisted,
I fume at myself, as I should have resisted.

I forgot to use my senses resisted all my fears,
Disconnected my heart, my eyes and my ears,
My poor prosthetic heart,
You ripped it and tore it apart.

BITTERNESS

For my love, there was no strategy,
I simply gave the best of me.
If I close my eyes, you appear in my head,
I still see you lying on my bed.
My bitterness towards you has no ending,
I hope you receive the thoughts that I am sending.

For you, I would have broken every man made law,
Now I look at you, I cannot believe what I saw.
You are the original Mrs. Jekyll and Hyde,
So beautiful to face but so evil inside.
My anger, sadness and loneliness,
Is only surpassed by the fact that you made me homeless.

Since I met you, my heart you have been messing,
To the heavens, I no longer give my blessing,
I wish the day my heart is no longer your slave,
I beg for the day I could dance on your grave.

When we met,
You shopped at cheap stores and I put fuel in your car,
I put you on a pedestal and made you a star,
I do not regret meeting you,
I just wished I had trusted you from a different view,
Will I ever trust another?
Not unless she is my sister or my mother.

As my bitterness unfolds with each breath that I take,
Now I realise everything about you was fake,
My poor prosthetic heart,
When you left, you tore it apart.

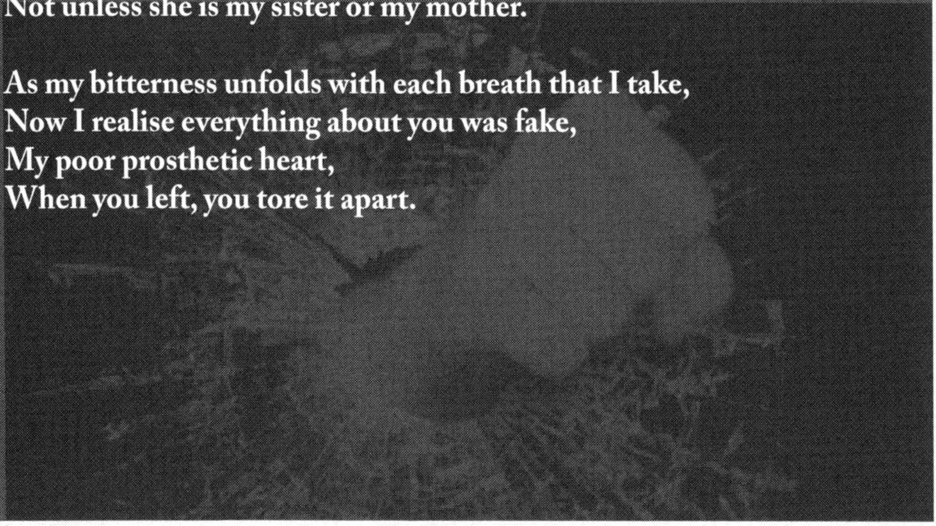

A MOTHER'S LOVE

It is a wonderful thing to have a Mother like you,
Whose love is so strong and love is so true,
So much of me is so much of you,
A single parent who doubled up into two.
Mother and Father rolled into one,
Early to rise, four or five when your day began.
Late nights, twelve to one when you closed your eyes,
In the morning, first to rise.

You worked so hard to keep us close,
Even when money was tight, we were still better than most,
Two or three jobs in a single day,
But you still had time for us all to pray.
Did not spare the rod when I needed to be told,
Now I understand I am a little bit old.
Must have been hard to keep four boys in check,
I smile recalling many times your hands around my neck.

The warmth and love you gave us then,
Helped us to grow from daughter to woman from boys to men.
Brought us up as children but as humans first,
To see the goodness in people not the worst.
Your love and example stand as a beacon in my life,
I disregard my struggles and my daily strife.
Thank you for always being there for me,
For that special love, you have always given so free.

A MOTHER'S LOVE

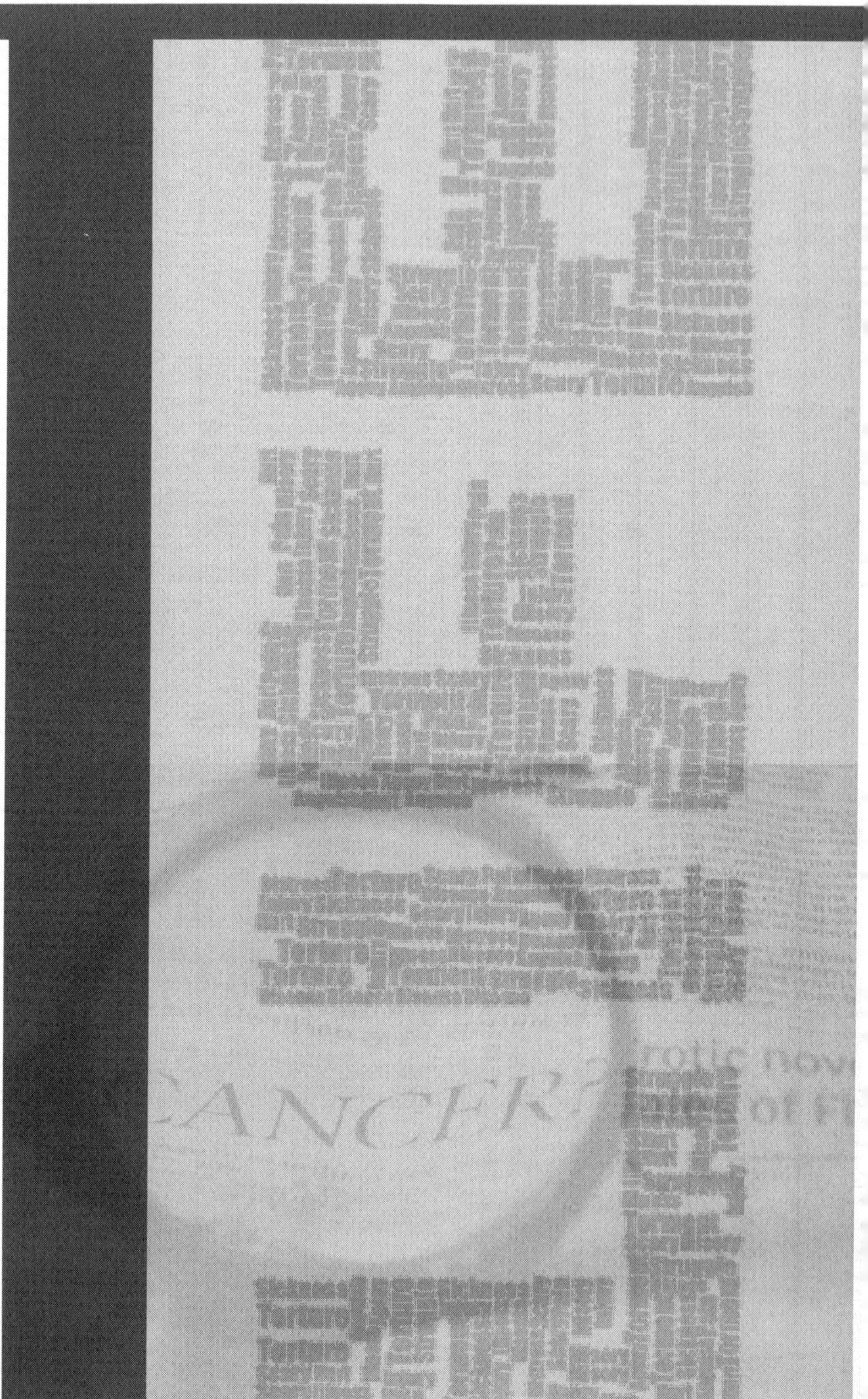

4

Life Unfolding

PART 4

LIFE UNFOLDING

DEPRESSION

I do not bite,
How I wish the world would see my true intention,
Not the fame that I am I may carry to my early grave,
No wealth could not save me from my sunken thoughts.
With so much confusion and uncertainty,
My mind gravitates to some kind of lunacy farm,
Unsure of the number of houses in my name,
I only sleep sometimes in one bed at a time.

Why is the silence in my head so loud?
I hear voices screaming and shouting,
Yet they are silent.
In my head, there are so many chambers,
I have visions I cannot see,
Things I can feel but I cannot touch.
In the Father, somehow I do believe,
I cannot express my will to live.

DEPRESSION

I reach from the fragments of my distorted mind,
I scream but no one hears,
I look but no one sees,
I walk, but on my two feet I cannot stand,
I can float but I cannot swim,
I visualize things you cannot dream,
In life, I see no beauty,
Just lacerations of scars.

I know you look and see the deception of my wealth,
If you look in my eyes, you will see the demons of my heart.
In truth, I have enormously bad days,
But a hug or hello can make day worth living again.

I AM CANCER

I am cancer
I create fear, panic and dis-illusion,
I seek sorrow, misery and fear,
I leave destruction and sadness in my trail,
I have no remorse.

I seek comfort in the misery of others,
There is no respect for the young and the old,
The strong, the weak,
For a beautiful wife,
For a dutiful son,
For the caring daughter,
The willing father,
I create unrest, havoc and fright,
At my worst, I am at my best.

I AM CANCER

I may invite myself into a family's home,
Before I leave, I might take one or two,
I am the lingering unrest that never really goes away,
I am not easy to go and will fight to stay

If I return, I will be stronger than before,
Nowhere is ever safe from me,
Look for me in the lungs and the heart,
The kidneys, bones and brain.
I stand strong, and I stand-alone.
I fear no one.
I am a law unto myself,
I am cancer!

RODNEY

A DEDICATION TO MY FRIEND FRANKLYN RODNEY WHO DIED TOO YOUNG

It has taken me many years,
I shed buckets full of tears,
Your loss has left many questions in my life.

I do not know where a rainbow goes,
Hard to accept you are no longer here,
I do not know where the sun hides at nights
I do not know where the moon sleeps at light,
I believed you would always be around,
Together stride by stride,
I do not know what holds the skies from falling,
The endless days and restless nights,
Only serves to remind me how much I miss you,

When you left, did you go to a better place?
We were all broken
Forced to put together our broken lives,
My guilt of living pursued me for so many years.

My biggest joy was having and loving my children.
But my biggest regret was not seeing you achieve the same.
Though you have been gone for so long,
I can still see your face in every blink I make,
In my life, I have been lucky; I have known real love,
I still miss you, the missing link I am always thinking of.

I have worked out that it is the sky that makes the ocean blue,
But when, when will I stop missing you?
I just took for granted we would grow old together,
Guess it's your legacy; I'm going to love you forever.
Your presence has been with me through the tears and the years,
Memories of you laughing at the bottom of my stairs,
Over something stupid, I did again.

RODNEY

Artistically gifted and embarrassingly handsome,
Confident with charm and a young Sidney Poitier lookalike.
He had the world at his feet,
Girls adored him and men admired him.

At school, I was the fighter, the no nonsense one,
He was the charmer, he was calmer,
He was never picked on,
He was my brother,
He was my best friend
We laughed, drank and we partied
Then you were gone
You broke your neck and you departed,
I broke my neck and I remained.

You missed my wedding and my first birth,
I have missed your wedding and your first birth,
Although you have been gone, my life has not all been bad,
I still think of you every day and of those memories we had,
You're the biggest loss my life has ever known,
I take your memories with me to a new city or to an old town.
I made you promise years ago,
I kept it, your name will be known.

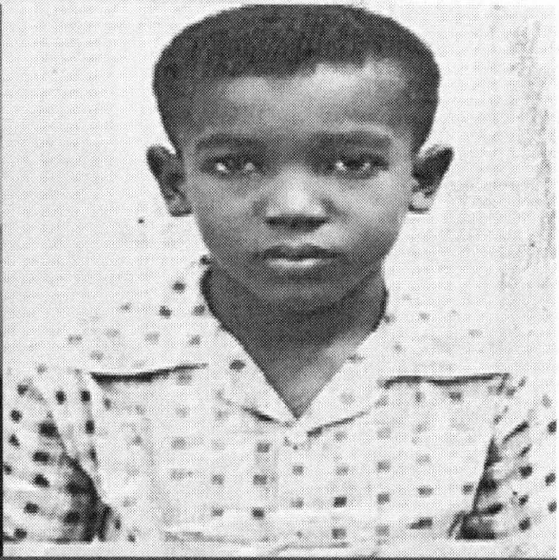

SARAH & JENNY

To the doctors, nurses and staff,
I owe you my eternal gratitude,
Moments when I was angry and close to being rude,
Feeling let down, nothing left to lose,
Which voice do you listen to?
Which one do you choose?

Shunted from pillar to post,
Trying to explain yourself,
You've done your most
When no one listens and it is coming to a crisis
You hold your thoughts,
Bite your lips and try to act the nicest,
When you feel frustration and anger is swelling inside,
You know yourself these feelings you must hide.
Discomfort and pain, hard to appreciate,
The sun always rises.
Then sometimes you get lucky,
As angels come in different guises.

Through luck and another fiasco,
I met mine in Jenny and Sarah.
Impossible to explain how they made my life much clearer
Daily visits, long hours on wards, I have gained some insights,
Misinformation, confusion,
Too many sleepless nights.
Actions are needed and correct information to be told,
If I can express my feelings, then I can only pity the old.
As for me, I am much more stable,
Cannot yet do handstands, run or jump,
Life is getting better I am much more able.

SARAH &
JENNY

TO HELL AND BACK

They praise me and tell me how strong I am,
I believe I am lucky not to be pushing up daisies today,
I am not saying they are all wrong, I did not hear my tune;
I did not hear my playing song.

I was given birth right as a fighter,
I was not ready to meet the one,
The only one to me who is mightier,
Broken neck or not, from the crash I survived,
From the pain, I knew I would struggle,
I am happy, I can feel the pain, I am alive.
I am not crippled from head to toes,
I have battled demons before,
So I will add this in my list of foes,
My right shoulder is also ruptured,
Now I know at times I am not the most cultured,
But for f... sake that pain took me to hell,
If you saw the look in my eyes that pain was easy to tell.

Hospitals became my second home,
Test upon test and I am wondering,
When will they leave me alone?
Took so many tablets,
I rattled as I walked,
Did not get much help from the officials,
No matter how long I talked.

TO HELL AND BACK

I am still trying my best to live my life,
Then I was cut with words like a jagged knife.
Then a man sitting before me said, "Could you please take a seat"
When I was told, I had cancer he did not need to repeat.
I got the broken neck, the shoulder and now cancer too,
I asked how do I cure this, just give me a clue.
One-step a time I was told,
This was the time I needed to be bold,
The pain I am living with took me to hell
If you saw the look in my eyes, it was easy to tell.

Back and forth, hospitals every day,
Pain, misery and discomfort in so many ways,
Seated in another hospital I have just been told,
You are pre-diabetic, now to me that is cold.
Family and friends took it in turns to be there for me,
No need to moan or complain
That is how it was meant to be.
I returned to the gym,
I heard people saying" look at him struggling, look at him",
I struggled to run, I struggled to walk but I knew I had to fight,
I believed that one day I would see a brighter light.

The tablets that I took allowed too many tears to flow,
The tears did not make me weak, they made me grow,
Cancer treatment booked and done
I was told "you could go home to your bed tonight hon",
Bathroom scenario was not fun,
The neck is still not perfect, but for me it is not an issue,
I certainly do not walk with a packet of tissues,
All the pain has gone from my shoulder,
You should see how I walk, so much bolder.
I believe life is an obstacle course,
Fight each challenge without fear, intimidation or remorse,
See the pain will remind you that you are still living today,
Do not be too proud to look to the man upstairs and pray.

The pain that I was living in took me to hell
If you saw the look in my eyes, it was easy to tell,
Now and then a little smile I crack,
Because I believe, I have been to hell and back.

blues
misery
mourning
despair
pain
woe
loss
sorrow
melancholy
sadness
suffering
agony
grief
heartache
letdown
anguish
depression
heartbreak
disappointment

Printed in Great Britain
by Amazon

62469185R00095